Through Grief

The Bereavement Journey

ELIZABETH COLLICK

Foreword by Claire Rayner

There is no way round grief,
only a way through.

DARTON · LONGMAN + TODD

Published in association with

D0784797

Published in 1986 by
Darton, Longman and Todd Ltd
1 Spencer Court
140–142 Wandsworth High Street
London SW18 4JJ

Reprinted 1986 (twice), 1987, 1988, 1990, 1991 and 1993

in association with
Cruse: The National Organisation
for the Widowed and their Children
Cruse House, 126 Sheen Road,
Richmond, Surrey TW9 1UR

First published by Mirfield Publications 1982
This revised extended edition © 1986 Elizabeth Collick

British Library Cataloguing in Publication Data

Collick, Elizabeth
    Through grief: the bereavement journey
    1. Bereavement
    I. Title
    306.8'8   BF575.G7

ISBN 0–232–51682–0

Phototypeset by Intype, London
Printed and bound in Great Britain by
Page Bros, Norwich

Contents

Acknowledgements

My special gratitude is due to: Margaret Torrie MBE, the Founder of Cruse, the national organisation for the widowed and their families, to whom many of the bereaved owe so much; Claire Rayner for her generous Foreword; Agnes Whitaker, of the staff of Cruse, for her advice and kindly encouragement; Darton, Longman and Todd Ltd for their ever-ready help; and all with whom I have shared grief and who have allowed me to make use here of what I have learnt from them.

ELIZABETH COLLICK

In glad memory
W.L.B. R.C. M.E.V.

Foreword

Only the unloved and unloving escape grief. It is the price we all have to pay, eventually, for the love that makes our lives worth the living. Whether it be the loss of parent, of spouse, of child or of brother or sister or friend, the pain lies in wait for us. And when it comes it has to be experienced before it can be eased.

For the majority of us death is a fact of life we'd really rather not think about, thank you very much. When most of us hear of others' grief we shy away from them as though they had some dreadful infection. Widows find that neighbours and 'friends' cross the street rather than meet them, that the polite letters and flowers sent around the time of the funeral are followed by total silence, that the loss of all sorts of ordinary everyday human contact has to be faced as well as the much greater loss of the partner without whom they feel incomplete.

People behave like this not because they're cruel and uncaring, but because they are ignorant. In the so-called Good Old Days when death came sooner and more frequently to the average family than it does today, when modern medicine has learned how to keep death at arm's length for rather longer than once was possible, people knew about grief. They knew how the bereaved reacted to their loss, knew what was expected of them as neighbours. Those were the days of big funerals when passers-by in the street stood in silence with doffed hats to show respect, not so much for the dead as for the unhappy mourners. Now we hurry our dead off as fast as we can (have you noticed how some motorists hoot impatiently at hearses if they hold up the flow of traffic?) and expect the bereaved to get over their distress in a matter of days.

Well, they can't. Grief has to be worked through, and this

little book explains just how the process happens. It is invaluable reading, not just for those of us who would like to be able to be of more help to others when they are bereaved, but also for those of us who are sensible enough to prepare for the experience before it happens to us. As one widowed business man is reported in these pages as saying, 'Some contingency plans have to be made for all emergencies and death is no exception. One buys insurance against death, so why not plan the first moves so that at least they are less effort than if one has to think them out step by step or – what is more difficult – react to the varied suggestions of well-meaning helpers?'

That's what Elizabeth Collick's excellent book is – a contingency plan for all of us. I commend it warmly to everyone who has ever loved anyone enough to fear his or her death. And there can't be many people who don't fall into that category.

CLAIRE RAYNER

Introduction

Bereavement is not an illness though it might well be called a dis-ease, a disturbance of life's regular course that is profoundly painful and distressing. It is likely to be encountered by us all. At the time of suffering it is a bewildering and often very lonely and frightening experience.

Some expert study and research has been done by notable psychiatrists and therapists about grief and bereavement. Valuable material has been collated about its practical and social aspects. Courageous and moving accounts of their personal tragedies have been written by people who have lost husbands or wives or parents or children. Nevertheless most people have neither had nor wanted to have any interest in the subject of death and bereavement until they have come face to face with its impact personally and inescapably. In their tragic and sometimes sudden predicament they would surely find a little reassurance if they could understand something of their devastating inner upheaval and recognise their strange disturbing feelings and overwhelming distress as symptoms of a natural and normal human experience.

Listening to the bereaved, sharing with them individually or in groups, I am repeatedly impressed and encouraged by the comfort and relief that come through the simple expression of feelings, the release of pent-up tears and the uncovering of sorrow as they talk with those who want to listen. Their burden of unhappiness is lightened as they share in the bereavement experience of others.

Mourners may have no willing listener; they may feel they must hide their grief for the sake of others or because their social code does not expect them to show emotion openly. In a quiet one-to-one talk or the mutual exchange of a group they

1

recognise – often quite suddenly and unexpectedly – a feeling expressed by someone else that tallies very closely with their own, or hear of some outlandish experience that relieves the guilt of their own bizarre or uncontrollable behaviour. This brings a glimmer of understanding and hope that may be the first step along the road to acceptance of their new situation.

What is written here attempts to describe what many have experienced – as often as possible in their own words – in the hope that it may reach some who are in the present sorrow of grief and that they may be comforted. It does not seek to soothe, to allay their pain, but to bring support and strength to cope with it as they recognise in the experience of others the yearning ache, strange fears, the anger, guilt, frustration, loneliness and lostness which now overwhelm them.

It is written in response to requests from professional 'carers' – nurses, ministers, doctors, social workers and others – whose work brings them into contact with the bereaved. Many of them have come to realise their own lack of training and the dismal inadequacy of society's understanding of this situation.

It is written too with those in mind who are relatives, friends, neighbours, colleagues and acquaintances of those in this tragedy, and all who may at any moment find themselves so. Often those who want to help feel inadequate and unsure of themselves in the presence of another's grief.

I refer repeatedly to the need for understanding help for those in grief. I do so more confidently now than in years past because in the 'caring professions' there is more training and a growing awareness of the needs of the bereaved, and their problems are receiving more professional help from GPs, psychotherapists, ministers of religion, health visitors, welfare workers and others.

And too, in many areas there is a growth in community groups whose members come together to share and help to relieve each others' burdens; some of these groups have sought training in bereavement care.

Some national organisations are listed in the Appendix to this book. Local information about sources of help will be available from public libraries and Citizens Advice Bureaux.

I have drawn my material mainly from the experience of some four hundred of the bereaved with whom, individually or in groups, I have shared grief over the last seventeen years and from my personal experience of widowhood.

I write mostly of widows because they make up the great majority of mourners and therefore of those mourners whom I have known. In the Western World widows outnumber widowers by 4 to 1. This is because the average age of death for men is lower than for women, and also because men tend to marry women younger than themselves. The basic experience of grief seems not very different for widowers and the widely held belief that 'it's easier for men' is certainly mistaken. What differences there are, are due I think more to circumstances or to social pressure than to gender. Reading 'him' for 'her' will not significantly distort what is written.

Throughout the book for the sake of clarity I have restricted the use of the words 'bereaved' and 'bereavement' to mean the loss by death of a close, significant person. I have used the word 'bereft' with a wider meaning of deprivation.

Death and Bereavement

Death belongs to life. (RABINDRANATH TAGORE)

Death is a crisis for the dying and for the living for which both are usually wholly unprepared. Yet death is a fact of life of which we are all aware in spite of the silence and denial that surround it. Few think of it as a natural occurrence in life's normal pattern: preferably we do not think of it at all. Death rarely finds a place in the school syllabus which includes birth and sex, marriage and mating, conception and contraception. Usually there is no preparation for it nor much teaching about it in the churches as there is with baptism, confirmation and marriage. Surely our attitudes to death and to life would be less riddled with fears and anxiety, if we recognised death and talked and taught about it as a part of normal human experience. We might then be better prepared to accept it in the deaths of those we love. It is not a cruel fate for them or ourselves but – with conception, birth, puberty, marriage, mating, maturity and senescence – a natural event to be expected and accepted.

There are hopeful signs that attitudes are changing and some relevant books are now available that would be useful to both teachers and ministers.[1] There is still, however, great need for better understanding of this universal experience if we are to break through the defences which cause society to ostracise the bereaved and treat grieving as a sign of weakness.

The social taboo on the subject of death seems to be slowly lifting. More doctors are open with patients and their relatives, and are prepared to discuss the prognosis of fatal illness. In

4

hospices – small hospitals for the dying – there is no attempt to hide the fact of approaching death, and patients and their families are given the opportunity to discuss and prepare for it. This realistic approach offers much comfort and peace for the dying and understanding support to those who must soon be parted from them. A hospice environment is never likely to be available nor suitable to all who are terminally ill, but the influence of this humane and caring movement is increasingly evident in general hospital care. This more open and positive approach to death is filtering through the medical and nursing professions and both patients and relatives seem generally to be grateful for it.

Doctors are, however, still divided in their opinions and in the advice they give relatives. Some warn against telling the truth to the one it most closely concerns and friends often endorse this advice, probably because they are themselves influenced by unconscious or superstitious fears.

For those who have shared their joys and sorrows throughout married life, the attempt to hide the truth from the dying one must be an almost intolerable burden. Yet once one's partner becomes a patient, especially a patient in hospital, there tends to be a surrender of decision-making: 'Well, you can't go against the doctor, can you?'

Many regret their silence: 'It was the first secret I ever kept from her'; 'I think he knew, but he wouldn't let on to me.'

One whose wife was dying of cancer kept up a cheerful pose, planning a visit to a son in America which he knew would never be possible. His wife responded, apparently eager and assured. He woke one morning to find her dead beside him and came upon a letter in a drawer. It had been written three months earlier and in it his wife said she hoped so much she would be brave enough not to tell him she was dying although she longed to, but knew he would not be able to bear the truth. 'When she really needed me', he said, 'I chose the wrong way to help.'

There is plenty of evidence that those who have watched their loved ones gradually accept the fact of approaching death, and have been able to share some of their deepest feelings, have been better able to mourn and come to terms with their grief.

Widows speak with gratitude of husbands who showed concern not so much for themselves as for the family 'when anything happens to me'. 'He said to our Lily, "Look after your Mum; she'll miss me".'

They treasure the memory of quiet resignation and courage and even wry humour: 'Now just you learn to do that right before I'm gone.'

One widow told of her relief when her husband confided that he knew he was dying: 'It gave us the chance to put things right before it was too late.'

The decision to share the news of approaching death with the one we love is painful to make, but I have never met a widow or widower who regretted having made it. Within the shared pain of approaching separation may be found a new tenderness and richer togetherness as thoughts and memories, fears and hopes are expressed at a deeper level in sorrow, forgiveness, gratitude and love.

'It is incredible', wrote C. S. Lewis, 'how much happiness, even how much gaiety we sometimes had together after all hope was gone. How long, how tranquilly, how nourishingly we talked together that last night.'[2]

1. E.g. Katharine Milne, *A Time to Die*, Wayland Publishers, 1977.
2. C. S. Lewis, *A Grief Observed* (Faber, 1956), p. 14.

Life's Little Deaths

Heartbreak is life educating us. (G. B. SHAW)

Grief is the pain that arises from any significant loss, or indeed from almost any significant catastrophe. It is not confined to the experience of bereavement. In all grief we need to suffer its emotional pain, to face the reality of loss and gradually to accept the challenge of life's altered circumstances.

I remember now, though with a far deeper understanding than at the time when they happened, two very different involvements in others' grief. Many years ago as a young student teacher I watched small children arrive on their very first day at school. No strangers were allowed inside the iron gates which clanged shut, leaving mothers outside and small groups of bewildered five-year-olds inside, huddled together, bereft and most of them in tears. Thankfully we are today wiser and more sensitive to the emotions of small children and more understanding of grief. It was part of my job to comfort them and help them to grow accustomed to a seemingly hostile world, controlled by whistles and bells and grown-ups they did not know. Years later I found myself trying to help survivors of Dunkirk to cope with life after losing a limb. Those in each of these groups were in the throes of grief, undergoing its normal process of suffering the distress of separation and gradually accepting a new situation and adjusting to changed circumstances.

Throughout our lives we face situations of grief and loss through which we learn to come to terms with circumstances that we do not like but cannot change. Through these occur-

7

rences we grow, gradually, unconsciously, laying down a pattern of response that will tend to determine future behaviour. Children lose a favourite hamster, school children fail to make the first team or achieve university entrance, adolescents lose their current sweethearts, a young wife endures the bitter disappointment of an unfulfilled pregnancy, a couple find they can no longer live together, and many today suffer unemployment, redundancy and bankruptcy.

Only recently have we come to realise the trauma and grief that follow a stroke or the deep emotional wound that results from an amputation. The grief of these serious physical losses is closely akin to the grief of bereavement, and when a surgical operation involves removal of an organ whose function is reproductive – as in hysterectomy, mastectomy, and testicular surgery – the resulting grief is often particularly distressing and prolonged.

All loss-situations are grievous in some degree and as we experience them throughout our lives we gradually build up a pattern of behaviour for coping with their pain and distress. Those who as children and adolescents were disciplined to keep their feelings under stern control – 'Cry-babies grow up ugly', 'Big boys don't cry', 'Now, Son, you learn to keep your troubles to yourself' – these unfortunates will find it more difficult in adult life to cope positively with grief than will those who were encouraged to express and share joy and sorrow, anger and excitement.

The grief of bereavement – its stages of shock, yearning, anger, depression and acceptance – are emotionally no different *in kind* from the grief of other losses. The difference, and it is an immense difference, lies in the depth of the pain that death brings, in the upheaval it causes and in the fact that it is utterly irreversible.

8

The Grief of Bereavement

*If the object of pleasure be totally lost, a passion arises
which is called GRIEF.* (EDMUND BURKE)

Those who have lost someone deeply loved and those who have
made a study of bereavement know that it is one of the most
painful and disturbing experiences that anyone can suffer. Yet
in society generally there is a tendency to underestimate the
depth of this distress and to suppose that normal healthy people
should not 'give way' and should soon 'get over it'. There is
often pressure on the bereaved, well-meaning pressure, to 'snap
out of it', 'to give over crying or you'll tire yourself out', or
even 'to try not to think about it: it won't bring him back'.

Perhaps a young widower had the truth of it: 'You don't
know the half till it hits you.'

A 'stiff upper lip' is a cliché very often used to describe the
buttoned-up unnatural control of natural emotions. It may
perhaps be an acceptable feature in a military, formal or
professional setting, but it is a very damaging one for those
who are grieving to assume or for others to ask of them. After
an RAF plane crashed on landing, killing all six of the crew,
the wife of the station commander called on one of the
bereaved wives, a young woman with a four-week-old baby,
and said: 'We service wives know what is expected of us, don't
we?' The young widow was the only 'service wife' who cried
at the funeral. When I visited her a fortnight later she told me
she 'had let everybody down, all his mates, the RAF *and* the
Queen'. She was ashamed to go out or show her face and

9

avoided her friends, 'creeping out to shop' only when most people were not about.

Slowly society is perhaps coming to recognise something of the misery and damage that this attitude imposes, but only slowly – for the well-being of the bereaved, far too slowly.

There is, I believe, a paradox about the pain of grief. It is this. Physical pain has some medical uses, but – I am assured – no healing properties, no intrinsic healing value. The medical and nursing professions see it as an important part of their job to eliminate pain as far as possible. Suffering must not be allowed if it can be alleviated. Pain is pernicious, unacceptable.

It is not so with grief. Grief needs to be suffered, deeply experienced and expressed. The loss that results from bereavement cannot be relieved or accepted except through the suffering of grief. The very pain of grief has within itself the power to heal; it is the way, indeed it is the only way, by which the bereaved come to terms with their loss. There is no way round grief, only a way through.

It is no kindness to the bereaved to help them to escape or avoid their grief. It must not be avoided, though mercifully it can be shared. A good friend or counsellor or pastor will create an environment in which grief can be expressed and sorrow shared, in which the mourner feels it is safe and acceptable to sob, to be angry, to cling or to reject, to curse or to pray, to rattle on with reminiscences or sit in depressive silence.

Just being there is sometimes the most helpful way of sharing grief, neither stemming nor encouraging tears or words, interfering not at all with what is going on within the mourner's heart, simply offering a caring presence and a listening ear and accepting that there may be little more one can do.

Grieving – grief work, as it has been called – is essential to future health and happiness. It is an individual process and a long one which cannot be hurried.

Nothing that is written here will be exactly true for every bereaved person. The substance of each section, the order of the sections, even the inclusion of any particular symptom or problem is no more than part of a generalised pattern of experience that is likely to be met with by most who grieve. Some

10

may pass unscathed through areas of grief which will hold others in acute distress for months; some will find themselves back in the painful emotions of the early days just when they believe themselves to be 'through it all'; experiences that are frightening to some can bring solace to others, while some can laugh at tactless remarks that will bring others to tears.

Mourners react to loss as the unique individual people that they are. The pattern of their grieving will depend on many factors: age and physical health; the relationship with the one who has died and the circumstances of the death; the behaviour that the family and society expect of them; and the ways in which they learnt to deal with stress and loss in early childhood.

Nevertheless there is within the experience a clearly discernible pattern; it is usually described in stages of shock and disbelief, of acute yearning, of depression and of acceptance. The progress is not straightforward, as the symptoms of the various stages overlap and intermingle, and there are regressions and sudden decisive steps forward, discouraging setbacks and temporary advances. Even after months or years one may find oneself jolted back into a state of dependency or depression or deep grieving.

The usual overall pattern, however, is of gradual recovery from shock and the protest of denial and disbelief, the upsurge of anger and guilt, the anxious fears, the searching and weariness of the time of yearning, through the sense of isolation, futility and loneliness of depression to an acceptance of loss, of a changed status and a life of new circumstances, interests and purpose.

Mourners often speak of a long dark tunnel; they are stumbling about in it, afraid of the darkness and the uncertain path. But tunnels have their endings when the darkness thins and there is first a glimmer and then a break-through into daylight. The very choice of this metaphor suggests that – at least unconsciously – the bereaved are expecting to find a way through.

There are some, however, for whom the path is particularly hard going and the outcome very uncertain. I have given little consideration here to the widowed who are survivors of 'unsatisfactory' marriages, chiefly because I have insufficient evidence on which to base facts or opinions, and I have found few

11

published works that are helpful on this aspect of bereavement against which to test my hunches. I quote from one below. One might expect that it would be less traumatic to lose someone with whom one had had a hostile or unsatisfying relationship. That is what the mother of a young widower thought: 'I expected him to settle down happily now that he's free of her and all that trouble.' But that is not how it generally seems to work out. The widowed I have known who have stayed with their partners in spite of unsatisfactory marriages have had more difficulty than most, not less, in coming to terms with their grief. It was very hard for them to be realistic about the relationship. Sometimes they felt resentful and at others were overwhelmed with guilt; sometimes they idealised the one who had died and at other times recalled – one might almost say unearthed – incidents that had caused much pain. In unhappy marriages there is much anger, often repressed, which leaves the widowed with a feeling of abnormal guilt. They have to work through their unresolved feelings and accept that the marriage was unsatisfactory, before they can deal with their grief. Only then can they find a new, acceptable status for themselves.

Lily Pincus, in her valuable and endearing book, *Death and the Family*,[1] writes of her work with marriage and family problems which led to a new concern with bereavement. She tells the stories of some of those who sought her help and writes that 'the responses to the loss of an emotionally important, loved person which emerge from these stories seem to be fundamentally the same as those we have come to understand as normal processes of mourning and grief. Any differences are only in degree.' For the unhappily married, however, who do not find such deep understanding and help as she offered, the course of mourning seems likely to be even harder going than for most, as she shows in the distress of those whose experiences she describes.

There are special difficulties also for those who suffer bereavements that follow one another closely. Acceptance of the first loss may be delayed and disturbed by emotions that are reactivated by the second death, which itself has to be worked through. A new wound reopens and aggravates the pain of one that has not yet healed. As with physical wounds, this may make for painful complications and distress.

An abnormal reaction sometimes occurs when a person is unable to grieve for one dear to her and is then faced with another death far less close, even perhaps of a pet or a character in a TV drama. The grief may be extravagantly excessive and appear utterly unreasonable, but the mourner will be expressing the painful feelings which would have been understandable but were suppressed or repressed at the time of the first death. Others may find this behaviour ostentatious and absurd – 'Fancy putting flowers on a dog's grave! I don't hold with such nonsense' – but for the mourner this may be a kind of second chance to experience the deep grief more appropriate to the earlier, really significant bereavement.

I have found a very marked difference of opinions and varying advice from doctors and friends about when the bereaved should be advised to go back to work after the trauma of the death of someone close.

One widow said that she went back the next day: 'I couldn't have borne it in the house. Work saved my reason.' Most of those in a small group felt this was rather precipitate: 'There was so much to do'; 'I couldn't have seen to read the post through my tears'; 'Whatever would people have thought!'

Most men and women are aggrieved that the time allowed for paid bereavement-leave is usually so short – it seems generally to be between two and five days, with an extra day for the funeral if it falls outside this allowance. The usual remedy is to ask the doctor for sick leave, but are they sick? Often not; and there is a feeling of resentment that it is necessary to resort to this pretext.

Some are aware that they cannot keep their minds on their work: 'I couldn't think straight'; 'I didn't really know what I was doing or what I had done'; 'My mates knew I hadn't done my share'.

Others work with a relentless intensity, determined to show that they 'don't give in'.

Those with whom I have discussed this – union officials, senior local government staff, doctors and others – generally consider that ten days' leave of absence after a close death

13

would be a reasonable allowance. It would certainly relieve pressure on some and be a benefit to most who are newly bereaved.

Bereavement is always a tragedy, but it is not a catastrophe. Most mourners come through and grow by the experience, often finding a deeper maturity and inner integrity, and a richer understanding and compassion.

1. Lily Pincus, *Death and the Family: the Importance of Mourning* (Faber, 1976), p. 14.

The Family

Every member of the family is to some extent bereaved and each will react both as an individual and as a member of the group.

The parent left with young children will have special problems in having to bear their misery and support them through their loss while she is almost unable to cope with her own. She may try to hide her grief and may even find that she cannot tell them what has happened. Sometimes children are hustled away to friends and great care is taken that they should know nothing of the funeral. Children a little older may hide their misery and try 'to be brave' for the mother's sake, perhaps assuming a cloak of nonchalance or exaggerated helpfulness. The whole family will profit if they are told the truth and given plenty of opportunity to share their grief, and most children will be helped to mourn positively if they take part in the funeral and are not protected from its sadness.

Children often need to be helped to express their feelings but some, even with understanding help, are unable to bring themselves to speak of the one who has died: 'He's never mentioned his Dad and runs from the room when I do'; 'We often talk about her, except the girl – she won't.'

It is often easier for children to talk to someone outside the family. It is never a healthy sign when they bottle up and cannot show their feelings. It is never true that they have none. The burden of unexpressed grief is one that no child should be allowed to bear. Some help must be found.

Certainly the children's school should be told of a near bereavement and it may be that some member of staff will gain a child's confidence. It was in fact a headmaster who was able to uncover and talk through the distress of the 12-year-old girl mentioned below. Children often behave badly at school and do poor work in this stress-situation. They are under great strain and have either to face or to avoid facing their grief while they come to terms with changed, insecure circumstances. It is surely not surprising if, in their bleak misery, they react with unresponsive discourtesy or exaggerated aggression, or seem unable to listen or work with concentration.

There is evidence of the likelihood of particularly severe stress in the relationship between a widowed parent and an only child, especially an adolescent only child who will already be undergoing the natural pressures of his or her age. A widowed father of teenage girls was 'told off by them for over-doing the affection' which they seemed to find in some way 'almost incestuous'.

A 12-year-old girl was so upset when she saw her widowed father cry that she refused to stay alone in the house with him.

A mother told of her distress because she could not stop hitting her 11-year-old son with whom she ordinarily had a very good relationship. She added with unusual insight: 'After all, it isn't his fault that he's the only man I've got now.'

There may be a suggestion that someone should take the child away for a while, but this can be felt as a rejection by the child and probably neither the parent nor the child will really benefit. Stress is not always best resolved by flight. There is much to be said for staying in familiar surroundings with recognised possessions and routine and among known friends, and sharing the family experience of grief.

In times of bereavement the tensions that are part of all normal family life are likely to increase and may become very disruptive if grief cannot be shared. Sometimes children, or even the parent, may seem to be holding their unhappiness tight within themselves, believing perhaps that it is weak to cry or that their self-control will make things easier for others. This sort of unnatural behaviour makes for added stress, too often because the grief that is not shared is unconsciously laid on the others. Over-stressed children in a bereaved family are sometimes carrying the burden of others' grief as well as their own. It is very important that tears should be allowed, even encouraged, and that unhappy feelings should be freely expressed. Shared grief strengthens family bonds and there needs to be opportunity and freedom for it. An evening 'talk-time', perhaps with a family friend or minister, is a valuable safety-valve in these difficult days.

A father has usually had less domestic responsibility, and in bereavement he will find it very hard to look after a family while continuing his work. Family help is usually the solution, but if he must cope both with running the home and going to work, he will probably need to remind himself that establishing a real understanding with his children is more important than good housekeeping. They will need a lot of support and a steady routine. Small treats, bedtime stories, encouragement with homework, sharing household chores, will help to lessen a child's feelings of loss and provide a close, loving relationship. There must be plenty of time for talk, for remembering mother and for sharing grief.

Some mothers, widowed while they still have a small baby to care for, seem to draw very great comfort from it: 'I loved her so much I couldn't put her down'; and a grandmother told of her very special closeness to the grandchild born three days before her husband's death. Such circumstances seem to help the expression of grief; they provide a new focus for feelings of tenderness and may give unconscious reassurance that although death takes away, life still goes on.

Those who have much-loved pets will readily forgive me if I include them in the family! Many children, and adults, have been comforted in their sorrow by being able to share the company of a favourite animal and show it tenderness and love. Incidentally, it is very often through the death of a pet that children first experience grief; they will learn more of the truth about life and death if they are given time to accept this loss before a new pet is introduced.

In-laws may be supportive or themselves need support, for they are also bereaved and the loss of a son or daughter seems against natural law and deprives parents of the sense of living

17

on in the lives of their children. The generation gap and differences in culture and domestic habits often make a close relationship with in-laws very difficult when the link between two families is lost, but where there are children there will probably be some pressure, if not some feeling of obligation, for the two families to keep in touch. Grandparents are rarely willing to surrender their grandchildren. On the other hand in-laws are often close and loving, able to help perhaps financially or by providing holidays or weekend breaks and the dead parent's father or mother may well be the one to become a substitute figure for the missing parent.

It is noticeable how often brothers-in-law and sisters-in-law are mentioned as being very helpful and supportive: they may assume something of the husband's or wife's place, taking over many responsibilities such as business matters, small house repairs and car maintenance, problems with the children and arrangements for the funeral.

Friends and Neighbours

Good friends and neighbours are a very great blessing to those who are caring for someone terminally ill and to the bereaved. Since they are not so close to the tragedy as members of the family they are able to support and befriend without such emotional involvement but with no less warmth.

During the last illness, whether at home or in hospital, practical help will be much needed and a friend who has given support in those worrying, exhausting days will have established a relationship that will be particularly welcome later on.

Nursing a very sick patient at home is an exhausting job. One may need to be available day and night. A friend who can sit with the patient perhaps for one night in a week, ready to call if need be, gives the one who is doing the nursing the chance of a night's sleep. This is such a valuable help that in some districts small groups of local volunteers have organised themselves to provide this service. It is greatly valued.

Those who are visiting hospital daily – or even twice daily – often at a distance, will welcome practical help such as laundry and shopping. Where there are children there will be even more opportunities, because children need a very stable routine in times of illness and stress, and a house without an adult around is particularly upsetting, especially when they come back from school to an empty home.

'Do let me know if there is anything I can do,' is not what is needed! A neighbour with commonsense and sensitivity will manage to find out when and how she can best help, and make a point of being regularly available.

In the hours and days immediately following the death the

bereaved should never be left to cope alone. There are so many practical decisions and formalities needing attention at this time of great shock and bewilderment. If there is no immediate family to give support, then someone who has built up a friendly relationship in the weeks before the death will be a friend indeed.

Many families do not experience a close bereavement nowadays until its members are in middle-life, and so they may not know what has to be done following a death. It will be useful if someone, preferably a friend, has found out in advance about procedures. Some relevant pamphlets and booklets are listed in the appendix at the end of this book, or the necessary information can be obtained by a visit or telephone call to a Citizens Advice Bureau. CAB staff are trained to give advice in these circumstances.

After the funeral and the family get-together there is usually a particularly desolate reaction. Sensitive friends and neighbours will find how best they can help; at first the chief need of the bereaved will probably be for a patient listener.

The sorting and disposing of the clothes of the dead is a task that most find really outfacing. There is no need for haste, but postponing it only seems to prolong a painful emotional resistance. Someone from outside the family will surely be a help in this dreary task.

And here are some other difficult situations in which friendly help would be specially welcome in these early days.

The first visit to a club or to church is much easier if it is not made alone.

The first day back at school is often difficult. A young child will need to be taken and put into the care of a kindly teacher. Older children will welcome the company of one or two close friends and this will need to be arranged beforehand.

Going back to work for the first time will be less embarrassing if it can be arranged to meet a friend. There will be looks of curiosity, even some shy avoidance perhaps, and it may be necessary to explain things to employers. A sensitive fellow-worker will be a great comfort at this point.

Anniversaries are difficult times – the birthday of the one who has died, the day of the death, their wedding day. And the first Christmas alone – indeed for many, every Christmas is a time of great loneliness, especially for the elderly. A friendly remembrance and perhaps a visit will be very welcome.

Holidays present a problem which may be eased by a kindly invitation to join a friend. Cruse, a most valuable organisation for the widowed, publish a Holiday List which gives addresses of a wide variety of holiday opportunities both for the widowed and their children.

During the dreary stage of depression the bereaved are often too low in spirit to want to join in anything and friends feel disheartened by repeated refusals and tend to stop asking them out. But do stick at it! This is a time when friends are desperately needed, even if it does not seem so. If they stay around, in time they will get 'Yes' for an answer.

The Funeral

The primary purpose of a funeral is the disposal of the body, but for most people its significance is much more than that and will vary greatly according to religious and cultural background, and personal and family attitudes. Most funerals in this country are carried out in accordance with Christian rituals. What follows relates to Christian tradition, but there is a growing number for whom Christian practice is wholly alien. There is probably no better way of learning about people of other cultures in a multiracial society than meeting them at a time of crisis and experiencing grief with them.

Many today who do not accept Christian teaching find a Christian funeral a mockery. There is no legal requirement for any funeral and there is, in fact, a curiously named crematorium arrangement for a 'non-Service service'. The British Humanist Association[1] publishes a secular service, but burial or cremation can be arranged without any service or congregation if that is the wish of the family or executor. When the body is to be buried rather than cremated, there is sometimes a wish for the grave to be in unconsecrated ground: this will not generally be available, and the matter should be discussed with the funeral director if feelings about it are important. When the body is cremated, the ashes may be scattered by the family or a friend, or some suitable place and occasion may be arranged by those responsible for the disposal.

All the practical arrangements for the funeral will be made by a funeral director. Funeral directors – they used to be called undertakers – are highly trained, experienced professionals, available day and night, who should be contacted as soon as a death has been medically confirmed. They will be in touch with clergy and crematoriums and will be able to take over all responsibility for arranging what the family feels to be appropriate. They are generally described by the bereaved as 'considerate', 'helpful', 'comforting and very understanding'.

The cost of a funeral is considerable: few of us have any idea of the labour costs and the detailed planning that are needed for even a very simple funeral and the bereaved are often unprepared for the expense which needs to be discussed and clearly agreed with the funeral director. There is often considerable embarrassment about this, an uncomfortable feeling that this is too personal a matter to be a business arrangement and that it is unseemly even to consider expense which is often in some way equated with regard for the deceased. It seems almost indecent to ask for an estimate, though members of the National Association of Funeral Directors always provide one. There is a tendency to overspend, natural but not sensible and quite unnecessary. It is wise to be open with the funeral director and avoid future shock and embarrassment.

Those with a firm religious faith who are regular members of a Christian congregation will have no difficulty in deciding with their clergy what is appropriate at a funeral. The family are likely to be well-known to the minister, who will be in sympathy with their wishes and share in making the arrangements. They will be supported by friends who share their faith, and in a familiar setting of religious practice and fellowship. For them the funeral service can be a profound religious experience of communion, love, grief, thankfulness, even joy.

So few rituals of mourning have survived in recent years that the funeral is almost all that remains to help the bereaved to grieve publicly and accept the mourning of their friends. It seems that for many the funeral takes place too close in time to the death for it to be personally very significant to those most nearly concerned. And the service is designed for those who profess a Christian faith, and neither the language – even in its modern form – nor the beliefs it enshrines are familiar or convey much meaning to others who are there.

An important aspect of the funeral is as a farewell. Many who are present have come 'to say goodbye', and the coffin seems to be the significant focus. Clergy have told of occasions of spontaneous reaction as the coffin disappears from view at a crematorium and the family and friends have waved and cried out 'goodbye', 'Goodbye, Mother'. On the other hand some who went to a memorial service for one whose body was given for medical research felt almost cheated because no body was there. There seemed to be a feeling that a service without a body was almost a farce, and the widow was aware of this uneasiness amongst her friends. Perhaps something of the sense of finality is lost when the body is not seen to its terminus.

And a funeral is a rite of passage, a formal public enactment of a deeply significant life-change. It gives the bereaved permission to grieve and redirect their lives and calls those who know them to acknowledge and respect their new status. The passing or passage of the dead body, its separation from the living spirit, is now made publicly evident and so also is the passing of the bereaved from the life they have known into a time of mourning when they must learn through grief to live the rest of their lives without the visible presence of the one they love and mourn.

At a meeting of some forty widows and widowers from a wide cross-section of society those present talked in small groups about the funerals of their husbands and wives, of their experiences, feelings and reactions, and readily agreed for what they said to be used here. All were at least nominally Christians and they discussed only Christian funerals. Some were recalling memories of many years past, others speaking of recent events. Much of what follows is drawn from what was said there.

At the time of the funeral the widowed themselves may be still in a state of numbed insensitivity:

'Your shock absorbers are still working and you don't feel much.'

'I was in a dream and rather enjoyed the music.'

'My feet were off the ground.'

'Should I have cried?'

Over 50 per cent of those at the meeting had been given tranquillisers by their doctors. They realised afterwards that this had increased their lack of response, 'blanketing out' their feelings and robbing them of an experience and of memories that they might have treasured.

Some, aware of themselves as the centre of interest, felt called upon to act a part that did not fit with their genuine feelings:

'I wasn't thinking of myself at all, mostly wondering who was there and what they would be feeling.'

'It's the one day you don't care or feel for yourself. You keep going for others.'

Some wanted to cry and could not; others cried and felt they should not:

'Shoulders back, head up, mustn't let the side down.'

'I had to behave well for his sake.'

It seemed that most felt behaviour was what mattered.

Except for those who were regular members of a congregation only a minority of the bereaved were visited by clergy before the funeral. None was offered an explanation of the funeral service though some would have appreciated this; a few were asked to join in prayer. There seemed to be a strong feeling that these visits were for the benefit of the minister 'so that he can find something to say about him at the funeral'. Some clergy, though not all, are willing to let a member of the family or a friend pay a short tribute to the deceased, and some felt this was more appropriate than a funeral address from one who did not know the one who had died.

Generally the visit from the clergy was valued not so much for its religious significance or support as for the sense it gave of personal concern.

Of those at the meeting mentioned above less than 25 per cent were visited by clergy after the funeral. These visits were particularly welcome as the bereaved felt great loneliness and despair, almost abandonment, after the funeral:

'I felt weighed down when they'd left; this is for ever I told myself.'

'As I shut the door behind them all, I was quite alone and then I broke, I really broke.'

In large urban areas it must be difficult, if not impossible, for ministers to visit the bereaved regularly or frequently. This is surely a great loss of opportunity, a loss both to the churches and to the bereaved families. Grief is a time of real need for caring ministry and invitations to fellowship for both children and adults. In some areas where professional ministry is over-stretched and not readily available small groups of lay people have undertaken regular visiting and befriending of the bereaved. An increasing number of such groups are seeking simple training and are now finding themselves very welcome in their communities.

Mourners often ask about 'viewing the body'. Should we? Must we? This usually entails a visit to the funeral director's chapel of rest after the body has been prepared and before the coffin is closed, though sometimes the body stays in the home until the time of the funeral. In some parts of the country viewing is an accepted part of mourning ritual. There is some evidence that those who have had no contact with the dead body may find it more difficult later to accept the reality of the death, and the widowed often mention the look of peace on the face of the dead. Some, on the other hand, find this practice abhor-rent and recall it later with distress or revulsion. This is surely a matter of individual choice for those most nearly concerned.

A gathering of family and close friends for a meal together has more significance than is perhaps immediately obvious. It brings together after the funeral those who have known and loved the one who has died, and this gives positive support to those members of the family who are most deeply concerned. It also gives opportunity for family reminiscing, which revives and strengthens family bonds and perhaps renews past relationships that have not been close for some years.

From everyone involved in the funeral the bereaved need above all a very personal consideration. Where there is resentment later, it is almost always because there is felt to have been some lack of sensitive individual courtesy – the late arrival of the minister, a mistake or mispronunciation of the deceased's name or no mention of it at all, a hurried assembly-line atmosphere at the crematorium or the untimely delivery of the ashes.

The funeral, whether it is a religious ceremony or not, witnesses to the fact that death is present in the midst of life, part of its pattern; it declares that the one who has died is a person who matters, significant both in the community and in his family circle; it speaks to the bereaved of personal sympathy and continuing concern.

1. The British Humanist Association, 13 Prince of Wales Terrace, London W8 5PG.

The Early Days

I am still in a state of shock – and the dark speaks from every avenue. (CHRISTOPHER LEACH)

SHOCK

Shock is the normal reaction to any bad news and is usually the immediate response to death or the news of the death of someone significant. It is a mental, emotional and physical reaction and can vary enormously in its effect from passive unresponsive lack of understanding to severe physical collapse needing medical attention.

Bad news should always, if possible, be broken in personal contact rather than by telephone or cable and it is wise to make sure that the one who has to be told is sitting down. People usually need time to take in what has been said and may just sit, as though they have not heard or do not understand; if they are alone when someone dies, they may be unable to take any action for minutes or even hours.

When describing shock the bereaved usually talk in physical terms:

'It was like a stunning blow: I thought the doctor had hit me and I shouted at her to stop, but they told me I never said a word.'

'I just went cold, like ice inside.'

'I walked away, but my legs weren't my own.'

'I remember most the hammering in my head. I couldn't hear or think for it.'

Those close to the dying may experience shock before the

actual death, perhaps when they are told the prognosis or suddenly realise for themselves how ill the patient is. It is a terrible experience to be told or become aware that a husband or wife is soon going to die, especially if one is told by a busy GP with a crowded surgery when one only went for a repeat prescription: 'It was like when I was in an earthquake and everything shook all round and inside me.'

A woman bought her husband a new pullover: 'It was grey and when he put it on I saw he was just the same colour. I found myself shaking and my teeth chattering so that I couldn't speak to him. I knew then.'

It may be that this early reaction, by anticipating the event, lessens the shock at the moment of death. It rarely, if ever, prevents it.

When the death occurs away from home, perhaps at work or in a road accident, so that the partner has had no opportunity 'to say goodbye', it may be very difficult to get the bad news across: 'His tea was on the table and then I heard the door and the police came. I said "No, no, it must be next door" . . . but it wasn't.'

If the death is sudden or violent, shock is likely to be more acute, and when a body is badly mutilated the horror can be so severe that people may react with physical shock even years later when the memory is revived.

Identification of a body is a legal requirement and can be a very traumatic experience. Where there is gross injury it is clear from what is recalled much later that it should not be undertaken by close family members on their own, as the shock of this duty may cause long-lasting distress.

Shock is sometimes delayed, perhaps for weeks, especially when the bereaved busy themselves compulsively or assert a tense stoical self-control: 'Don't fuss over me. I don't crack.'

Later when the shock can no longer be absorbed, it will surface and be difficult both to recognise and to treat.

A widowed father drew attention to the difficulty of diagnosing shock – and therefore of treating it – in children, who often 'get over the physical shock remarkably quickly'.

29

This is a time when people need caring support, and where this is not immediately available from family or friends there would seem to be a responsibility on those who have had professional care of the patient – the hospital staff or medical social worker, district nurse or GP or the police – to inform and involve the help of the statutory community services or the local church or some appropriate voluntary organisation to sustain the bereaved in their distress and help with immediate arrangements. No one in this situation should be left to cope alone.

Many people refuse to think about death until it comes very close and cannot be escaped, but much distress could be avoided if some sensible forward planning had been done. 'Some contingency plans', said a widowed businessman, 'must surely be made for all emergencies and death is no exception. One buys insurance against death, so why not plan the first moves so that at least they are less effort than if one has to think them out step by step, or – what is more difficult – react to the varied suggestions of well-meaning helpers.' Clearly he spoke from experience.

NUMBNESS

The first impact of a close significant loss often deadens feeling. Whatever the psychological mechanism, I see this numbness as a merciful insulation from the intensity of acute emotional pain: 'I knew what had happened. I heard them arrive. "He's dead," I said to myself, but it didn't seem to matter. It was just a happening, nothing to upset myself about.'

The bereaved find it hard to describe this curious state, perhaps because its essence is a kind of non-feeling, almost of non-being. There is a great distance between them and their environment:
'It was like a dream, all happening but not real.'
'Everything was so far away that I wasn't part of it.'
'It was like watching a film, all other people doing it.'
'It's no good trying to describe it – I just wasn't involved.'
'It was like me watching them watching me.' It was in these words that a fifteen-year-old girl stammered out her feelings when she was reproved for not responding to those expressing

their sympathy after her mother's funeral. I find it a very poignant description of her sense of unrelatedness to what was going on around her – a vivid reminder of feelings that many will recall from those early days of bereavement.

This detachment brings a sense of strange unreality, as if a large part of the self is cut off and no longer involved in what is going on. A widow whose husband's death was expected had planned what she would do: 'I did it like an automaton. I was just a machine without any feelings, doing what it had to do.'

Another said, 'I seemed to be surrounded by a thick layer of cotton wool. Inside it, and only inside it, I felt safe.'

Within this insulated, isolated world the bereaved feel better able to preserve their sanity and cope with things, though probably not with people. The same kind of emotional defence is related by C. S. Lewis. Describing his experience after his wife's death he writes of a sort of invisible blanket between himself and the world.[1]

A widower said: 'For days after she died I had no room in me for anyone, not even for the children.'

Sometimes this suspension of feeling, the sense of being outside oneself, depersonalised, makes it difficult to talk or to listen, even to have any clear ideas of one's own or to take in other people's. Yet this is a time when urgent decisions have to be made. Though the bereaved may want to evade the pressures of decision-making, there may later be regrets, even recriminations and resentment, if things are now taken entirely out of their hands. Most will need patient help, perhaps repeated questioning and explanations, but rarely total direction even when they ask for it.

This is of course a very difficult time for the bereaved; it is often an even more trying one for those who are supporting them.

DENIAL

A young woman went to visit a friend whose child had died in hospital the day before. She was greeted excitedly: 'I've been waiting all night, I knew you would come. Has the hospital phoned? I knew it was all a mistake.'

The visitor was bewildered and speechless. She remembered

31

that she had promised to take telephone messages from the hospital, but there had been none. Besides, the mother was with the child when he died. Whatever was this all about? It took some time as they talked for her to understand that the mother in her shocked distress had not fully grasped the fact of her child's death. She had sat up all night waiting to hear that 'the hospital had made a mistake'. This young mother, a sensible level-headed miner's wife, had coped efficiently and gallantly with crisis after crisis in the child's short life, but in her grief she needed this temporary shield of denial to defend herself until she could accept consciously the truth that was too terrible to believe.

A young man was with his mother when she died in hospital. He talked with a doctor and the ward sister and took away his mother's belongings, but he came back at visiting time the same evening and said to the Sister: 'I've just popped in to bring her some fruit.'

The fact of the finality of death is not easily grasped. The truth is only gradually absorbed. Often it is the funeral with its rituals and the presence of family and friends that provides the first jolt of truth:

'I didn't believe it till I saw him in his coffin.'

' "That's the end now, mother," they said as we left the chapel, and then I knew he had gone.'

For weeks widows may find themselves listening for his key in the door, jumping up to put the kettle on when they hear a car stop, turning to his chair to share a letter or a joke, even shopping or laying the table for two.

A widow described how she got up several times at her usual early hour and went down to the kitchen to cut her husband's sandwiches for him to take to work: 'It was only when his snack-tin wasn't on the shelf that I remembered he didn't need it any more.'

Another went up to the bedroom where her husband had lain ill before his death to share with him a cheque that had arrived for a piece of work that they had done together: 'My hand was on the door-handle and then I remembered the empty bed. There was no one now to share with.' She went downstairs and burnt the cheque: 'Stupid I know, but it was worth nothing, less than nothing.' Telling of this months later, she added: 'It was, I think, the most devastating moment of my life.'

In Mary Stott's poignant refrain: 'In grief we do as we must.'[2]

A daughter who went to see her widowed father on his birthday found him sitting beside the telephone: 'I knew Mother wouldn't forget it,' he said.

These incidents, small and not so small, catch people out unexpectedly. They are painful and bring tears and heartache, but they also help to heal grief, for they are a repeated, insistent reminder of the truth that has to be accepted and made part of inner consciousness; the dead are not around any more.

Another phenomenon which is perhaps part of the same process of denial is a sense of the presence of the dead or even the illusion of seeing them or hearing them speak:

'I saw him sitting in his chair and then my daughter said, "It felt as if Dad was with us just now". It was so real for both of us.'

'I woke and heard her cough and there she was, standing right beside me.'

To some people these occurrences seem to bring a feeling of comfort and warmth and peace, rather than distress, while others find them disturbing. In these early days mourners still feel very close to those from whom they have not long been parted and the presence of those they love seems all around. Whether they find these incidents frightening or comforting depends probably on their responses to imaginative experiences in early life. In either case, this sense of the presence of one who is not physically there is a normal experience in grief, not only in bereavement but in any distressful situation of parting.

The bereaved are hesitant to talk about these fantasies because hallucinations, 'seeing things', are widely associated with mental instability: 'They'd say I must be going crazy.'

A doctor[3] who has made an intensive study of bereavement describes these experiences as entirely normal and quite usual, but rarely heard about simply because people hesitate to admit to them. Such feelings are not abnormal or extraordinary, but natural and typical for those who are having to cope with a tragic reality that they are not yet ready to accept.

Mourners are often worried and distressed by their unusual behaviour at this time and by their strange feelings and experiences. 'Am I going mad?' is a question that is often asked. The answer is a clear unequivocal NO, but it must not be left just at that. I am always glad when this question is asked; it needs to come to the surface so that it can be calmly and openly discussed. The fear of 'going out of my mind', of mental instability, 'having a breakdown' is not unnatural to those who feel their lives have been turned upside-down. When the fear is smothered because it is too fearful to face, it becomes even more frightening: 'You see, it *might* be true.' Those close to the bereaved, especially to those bereaved suddenly, should be ready to talk about this fear if there is the least hint of it. It is sometimes said lightly, but it is not felt that way. In a small bereavement-group the subject of 'Strange Feelings' can be a useful topic through which to open up fears and fantasies, and members are often willing, even eager to talk quite openly and are usually surprised to find that others share this fear. It is a great relief to most when the topic is raised and talked about, but those who are not able to face their problem in a group will perhaps feel readier to talk it over in a one-to-one situation when they realise that the fear of 'going mad' is not theirs alone.

1. C. S. Lewis, *A Grief Observed*, p. 7.
2. Mary Stott, *Forgetting's No Excuse* (Faber, 1973), p. 184.
3. Michael A. Simpson, *The Facts of Death* (Prentice Hall, 1979), p. 246.

The Heart of Grief

My heart and body are crying out, come back, come back. (C. S. LEWIS)

YEARNING

The most acute pain and deepest distress come in the days following the numbing shock of death and the activity and sense of urgency that mark the days before and around the funeral. Stunned feelings come sharply alive; the bereaved are overwhelmed with aching longing for their dead as the extent of their loss begins to come home to them. Their grief is almost totally absorbing.

Generally the experience at this yearning stage is of a deep groundswell of sadness with waves of acute emotional pain, bouts of harsh sobbing and sudden gusts of anger. There is a sense of bewilderment, of anxious questioning and guilt. Seemingly aimless activity alternates with aching tiredness and the mourner's personal predicament is the main, if not the only, interest. Thoughts and memories of the one who has died and the prospect of a lonely future sharpen and continually stimulate the pain of loss.

A widow was visited by her vicar some two or three weeks after her husband's funeral. She was unresponsive to his consolations, tense and tight-lipped, controlling her tears with difficulty. After a long silence he asked if there was anything he could do to help. Then she broke down and shouted at him: 'Yes, there is. Tell me what to do with all this bloody agony.' His answer was a simple question: 'Do you think you could share it?'

Her tension and efforts at self-control and her sharp outburst of angry appeal are typical of the sort of reaction that visitors may meet in this early phase. It takes loving understanding and patience to accept, but it is a sign of trust when the bereaved feel able to reveal the inner hurt which so distresses them.

During this time of acute grief the mourner's chief concern is with the one who has died. She has little time or energy for anything else. Her deep need is to grieve, to re-experience the past, recognise that it is past and begin to look towards a future. But the past is still very much present, and a large part of her is still involved with the person with whom she shared her life, its sorrows and joys and plans and daily happenings. He is not yet dead for her:

'I can't think of life without him, I mean, I just can't believe he's gone.'

'I keep thinking he's around . . . and then . . .'

'When he doesn't come in from work, I go to the door to look for him.'

'Sometimes I went to meet her bus . . . She was never on it. I went home with a stone in my heart.'

At the same time the mourner is involved in a strange new present life in which established habits seem to have no purpose:

'Why get up? No one needs me.'

'I can't cook a joint just for me.'

'I don't turn the telly on now there's no one to laugh with.'

And then there's the future; that needs to be faced, planned for, but planned for without the one who has always shared the planning.

This jumble of time is confusing, and part of the work of grief is to come to terms with the reality of the past, to accept and take control of the present and look towards a future. It is very hard, painful work.

There are often physical symptoms too; headaches and other stress symptoms, various aches and pains, probably more trouble with any existing medical problems, a loss of appetite, aching tiredness and, perhaps most common and intractable, sleeplessness:

'My heart's a ton weight and my chest just aches with it.'
'I try to eat but nothing has any taste, not even the beer.'
'My feet are like lead to drag around.'
'I've a dreadful pain behind my eyes when I want to cry and can't.'

Mary Stott[1] writes of 'a searing pain somewhere in the guts' and of 'quite terrifying physical exhaustion' at the rigid self-discipline needed to control her tears in public.

For some, sleep may be such a blessed escape that they do not want to wake or get up, and prolong their hours of dozing far into the day. Others long to sleep but changed circumstances break established habits and patterns, and anxiety increases tension: 'I'm tired through the whole day, but the nights are worse.'

The widowed no longer have a bed-fellow and the sleepless nights are long and lonely. And for some there are nightmares, particularly disturbing to those who have never suffered them before: 'And when you wake shivering – well, you're alone.'

This yearning stage is the phase of mourning that just must be worked through if life is to regain its equilibrium. There must be opportunity to mourn and courage to experience the loss for which grief is the only remedy in this time 'when so sad thou canst not sadder'.[2]

LOSS

The crucial factor in bereavement is not the death and the circumstances which surround it, but the loss and deprivation which result from it. Death has come; the fact is final, inescapable, but it has happened to someone else. The loss is irreparable, and it is with this loss that the bereaved must live. The cause of grief is the loss of a close significant relationship with a living person; the process of grief and mourning is the way by which the living come to terms with this loss, with all its emotional, practical, physical and spiritual consequences.

A widower was asked on his return to work to account for his two-day absence. 'I lost her Wednesday, buried her Saturday, now it's Monday and I'm here.' His bleak, unelaborated statement revealed rather than concealed the depth of his grief.

Friends speak and write in condolence letters of 'your sad loss', and the widowed when they are recalling the past, more often use the phrase 'when I lost my husband . . .' than 'when he died'. Perhaps to friends loss is a less stark, more gentle concept than death; to the bereaved, loss realistically describes their personal predicament.

Another expression which the bereaved use in speaking of their loss is '. . . when I was left', 'I was left last month'. This evocative phrase reveals an unconscious sense of having been abandoned.

The bereaved feel deserted, deprived, reduced, empty.

The word 'widow' is linguistically very close to words meaning 'empty'. 'I hate the word "widow",' one said, 'I associate it with spiders, weeds and Queen Victoria, never with myself.'

'Avoid the words "widow" and "widower",' a funeral director advised, 'They don't recognise themselves. It's not a word they like, not at all.' He was quite right. Nonetheless, like it or not, emptiness is an uncomfortably apt description of bereavement distress.

Johnnie was the first disturbed child with whom I was professionally involved. He was nine years old and motherless. One of his symptoms was that he stole and then gave or threw away what he had stolen. One day he rushed into the room of his favourite therapist with a new football which he dumped on the table and then, crying uncontrollably, he buried his face in the therapist's lap. 'Now I wonder,' she said, almost speculatively, 'just why you wanted that football.' After a long tense pause Johnnie jumped up. 'I've got a big, big hole right *here*,' he said, and thumped himself hard just below his ribs as he stamped round the room in angry frustration.

Johnnie's 'big, big hole' was an emptiness at least as big as the football; it could never be filled – not, that is, by anything but the love that he had lost.

I recognised Johnnie's pain some thirty years later in the hollow ache of my own heart. I have heard its echoes often since as the bereaved have tried to express their sense of desolation, though never quite so dramatically as when a group of widowed people were comforting an elderly man who had lost his wife only two or three weeks earlier. With a sad shake of his head he said, 'It's like a big empty hole right here,' and hugged his arms to his chest.

The phrase 'an aching void'[3] was coined by an eighteenth-century hymn-writer in a rather different context and, perhaps surprisingly, it crops up from time to time when the bereaved describe the inner emptiness and hollow misery of their hearts:

'I'm always hungry, but I don't much want to eat.'

'I go out every day, rain or fine – just window-shopping.'

'I'm ever so restless, can't sit still. I don't know what it is I want, but I keep getting up to get it.'

'I've got my work and my pipe, but it still gnaws at you.'

Some tragic encounters suggest that this particular aspect of the reaction to loss needs to be better understood by the community, for society places a very heavy burden on public figures who are applauded for 'carrying on with the show' when they are inwardly overwhelmed by private tragedy. Demands are made upon them which hamper grieving and deprive them of the time and privacy to mourn, and their efforts to live up to other people's expectations are destructive of healthy grieving and prolong the process.

When the aching hunger for someone dearly loved cannot be fully expressed, tolerated and accepted, there may be an unconscious attempt to satisfy this inner emptiness – this 'big, big hole' – in irrational and socially unacceptable ways. Over-eating and smoking may become compulsive, drink and drugs addictive, craving for something – anything – may drive those in this distress to gamble or overspend or cheat or steal. Shop-lifting, often quite unnecessary and out of character, is a not unknown symptom of delayed or repressed mourning.

If the grief that should relieve the stress of loss is checked, bottled-up or repressed, the pain of loss becomes unbearable. Even years, many years later the bereaved who have not been able to come to terms with their unhappiness react in ways that are beyond their control, bring no real relief, and are not generally recognised as a desperate effort to cope with an intolerable situation. Those in this distress need the help of professional therapy or trained, experienced counselling, but too often neither they nor their family, friends, doctors nor ministers recognise their problem.

It is in the early weeks and months of bereavement that this empty, hungering aspect of grief needs expression and supportive understanding, even when – indeed, especially when – there appears to be complete composure, self-sufficiency and self-control.

Give sorrow words: the grief that does not speak
Whispers the o'erfraught heart and bids it break.[4]

A counsellor who worked with the bereaved used to ask them to list the losses that the death they were mourning had brought them in order to help them to uncover some of the depth of their loss.

The lists usually started with losses that were obviously practical or related to new roles which the widow or widower now had to take over – father or mother to the children, chief breadwinner or cook, handyman, painter and decorator, gardener, shopper, banker, motor mechanic, etc. The most urgent of these roles were those that the survivor felt least able to fill, or which by incompetence within them had led to embarrassment or catastrophe.

A widow whose husband had always looked after the car did not know that its engine needed oil; a widowed father found shopping and packing up his children's lunches a very daunting daily chore; the widow of an accountant had never written a cheque and was at a loss how to pay her gas bill. Unaccustomed jobs, even if small, loom large to those under stress. One realises in the bereavement situation how valuable it would be if both sexes had learnt to cook and mend, to drive the car and handle a screwdriver!

Deeper feelings are involved in the loss of the relationship itself. Parents have lost a part of themselves as well as a guarantee of their own continuity. Children will have lost their closest bond, their protector and provider and, with these, their sense of security. The widowed have lost the one with whom they shared home and family, their social companion, their

40

sexual partner, their confidant/e and comforter – this last, a specially poignant loss at this time of distress.

And lost relationships result in loneliness which is such a central element in bereavement that it will be more fully considered later.

Another aspect is the loss of a pattern of life. Widows whose work has been in their homes have been used to planning the day so that it goes smoothly for the two of them – housework done, meals on time, ready for the evening at home or out together. Now planning seems futile and there is a purposelessness about life: 'What's it all for? It's pointless just for me.'

A widower told of his almost daily sense of panic as the time to leave work approached: 'There was nothing to go home for. Where to go? What to do? My sister's? The pub?' There were hours to fill, burdensome futile hours. He had lost the one who gave life purpose and made it worth living.

Although for those with children still at home there are now many problems and added responsibility, this generally seems to help. The routine has to be kept going, the children's needs met and family life sustained. The burden may be very heavy, but there is a sense of continuity, a stabilising pattern to life. While children are around life is rarely dull or pointless.

Loss is the sad refrain of the bereaved. They are both loser and lost.

There is a real sense in which the death of someone close and significant is a death of a part of the self:
'When she died, I lost a bit of my*self*.'
'There's nothing inside any more to make me tick.'
'I've no heart for anything.'

As a funeral party were leaving the graveside, a young widow clung to the minister crying: 'Don't leave me. I don't want to go. There's a piece of myself you've buried. Let me stay.'

A girl of fifteen whose mother had died, went off to school the next day and was found, dazed and bewildered, wandering round the playing-fields. Again and again she repeated: 'I'm just lost, lost. Yes, I know where I am, but I'm lost. I'm sort of looking for something, I think – a bit of me.' To use an apt phrase, 'she really wasn't all there'.

And many have lost their map. 'It's a strange world, isn't it? Like being in a town you don't know and no one to show you the way.'

It is crucial to recovery that the lost should find a good guide.

SEARCHING

Whenever we lose something of value, something important to us, something essential to the smooth running of our lives, or simply something that is what we are accustomed to use in a particular situation, we search. The key of the car or the house, our wallet or handbag, our diary, our favourite screwdriver or a kitchen knife, the dog or a child in the supermarket – if we lose anything we value we become anxious, irritated, frustrated: 'Where on earth is it? It must be somewhere. I *must* find it'.

We not only search, but search and search again in places where we have already failed to find. We are restless, moody, unable to concentrate or settle down. 'After all, I just might have missed it.'

Failure to find also makes us angry, perhaps with ourselves for our carelessness or with someone else whom, justly or unjustly, we blame: 'She's moved it again'; 'Why couldn't the child wait where he was told'. And so it goes on until we find or resign ourselves to the loss or make do with a substitute.

The bereaved have lost someone infinitely significant for whom there is no substitute. They have this urgent restless need to search and to find; their searching is natural in their loss, but it cannot succeed because the object they seek is a living person. The one they so desperately need to find, for whom they must search and search, is the one they know and love. They seek the living; their search is vain because the one they love is no longer alive.

I did not identify the need to search nor recognise this searching element in my own bereavement behaviour until some years after my husband's death when Dr Murray Parkes' book[5] about bereavement was published, in which this important aspect of grief is so clearly and convincingly explained. 'In social animals,' he writes, 'from the earliest years, the principal behaviour pattern evoked by loss is searching.' It would

42

perhaps be naive to think that I should have escaped much pain and bewilderment if I had read this book at the time of my loss, but I remember my relief and gratitude when, years later, I recognised the relevance of this need to search to some of my hitherto inexplicable and embarrassing behaviour.

A week after my husband's funeral I drove from Sussex to Yorkshire to share my grief with a much loved friend, and had planned to drive on to others for the night. En route I dropped in to the beautiful medieval church in the village where we had started married life. I found it full of menacing ghosts and left in tears. I lunched at a restaurant where we had often enjoyed small celebrations, but the food choked me and I complained angrily. After my visit I stopped in a favourite picnic spot for coffee but felt so sick in body and spirit that I drove back home, forgetting that I was expected to spend the night in Yorkshire. I had searched in church, restaurant and lay-by; it is perhaps not surprising that I was too disheartened to go on.

I remember how, in the early weeks of bereavement, I rang my own telephone number from my own house and was angry that the number was engaged. It strikes me now, even as I write, that I was still 'searching', hoping – so to say – that the one I knew was not there would answer my call. Such incidents are typical of the strange irrational behaviour of those who are under the stress of searching for those whom they have lost, and who have not yet come to terms with their new situation.

I remember too six-year-old Anton, a Belgian boy who escaped to England with his parents during the Second World War. A week or two after his father's death he was missing from bed in the early hours of the morning and found digging a hole in the orchard. As he was being carried back into the house, whimpering like a puppy, he whispered: 'Maman will not tell me where is my Papa.' This Belgian mother, a lovable, sensible person, visited her husband's grave two or three times a day for several months; she returned so often to the ward of the hospital in which her husband died that her visits had to be officially banned. Six months after his death she was admitted to the same hospital for major surgery and there steadily regained her equanimity. After the war they returned to their own country where she reorganised and controlled her

43

husband's factory. These two – orphaned and widowed in a strange country, isolated from friends and family – had a more than usually bitter grievous search. Inevitably it was in vain, but both have since found serenity and healing.

In most everyday circumstances searching for what is lost is done quite consciously, but in bereavement more often the purpose and drive of this behaviour goes unrecognised. A doctor's widow, herself a doctor, found herself hanging about after a professional meeting, the last to leave. She felt perplexed and kept wandering round in the hall and offices and cloakroom. 'I suddenly realised I was waiting for Peter. I sat in the car and sobbed my eyes out. It was a long time before I was able to drive home – alone, of course.'

Mourners often find themselves searching faces in the street or at a meeting or as they shop, unconsciously half-expecting or hoping – well, perhaps not quite half – to find the one they mourn amongst the crowd. Mrs J.'s search had a more disastrous result than disillusionment; she jumped off a moving bus because momentarily she thought she had seen her husband walking home from his work. In the casualty department where she was taken for treatment she felt so ashamed that she would not explain why she had done this: 'They would have thought I was mad or drunk if I had said I thought I had seen my dead husband.' She was somehow made to feel irresponsible and unco-operative and was too embarrassed to keep a further hospital appointment. (One may wonder how understandingly her explanation would have been received had she made it.) Fortunately she plucked up courage to talk about the incident, and next day a widow who had been longer bereaved went with her to the hospital, ready to answer any embarrassing questions.

A widower, who had been accustomed to calling for his wife at her mother's house on his way home from work every Friday, found himself calling there even more frequently after his wife's death, 'Though I couldn't abide the old lady. It's as though I thought to find the wife there – I'll have to stop it.'

Another said: 'When I wake and find her gone I go downstairs to see if she's making a cuppa in the kitchen.'

To find oneself behaving unusually, irrationally, yet restless and frustrated if one tries to stop; not to know why one is doing what it seems one must do; to feel ashamed and foolish and unable to explain; to find no comfort or satisfaction from one's restless activity; this is a bewildering, frightening experience in an already distressing situation. When something of this concept of loss-and-search is understood, mourners are often relieved and comforted to discover that behaviour which seemed inexplicable, uncontrollable, senseless and disturbing, is a normal universal bereavement experience. This will not ease the urgent need to search, but it goes some way towards relieving the bewilderment and distress.

It may make, too, for more compassionate understanding from those around if they are able to recognise something of what lies behind this compulsive restlessness.

1. *Forgetting's No Excuse*, p. 183.
2. Francis Thompson, 'In No Strange Land'.
3. William Cowper, *Olney Hymns* 1: 'O for a Closer Walk with God'.
4. William Shakespeare, *Macbeth*.
5. C. Murray Parkes, *Bereavement: Studies of Grief in Adult Life*. Tavistock Publications, 1972.

The Bitterness of Grief

The heart knoweth its own bitterness. (PROVERBS 14:10)

ANXIETY

In a light-hearted conversation about holidays abroad an experienced traveller remarked that his worst moments were those when he was separated from his passport: 'I know really that they are going to give it back but it's the dreadful thought of what-would-happen-if . . .'

The anxiety of being separated from so essential a means of identification, something so necessary to one's security as a passport is bad enough. It is magnified many times in the anxiety that follows the loss of a close significant person, especially the loss in childhood of a parent or the loss of a marriage partner. Such a loss is an appalling threat to one's security and sense of identity and purpose. It undermines self-confidence, wholeness and happiness.

The anxiety of separation is an over-shadowing emotion in these dark days: 'As soon as I wake, there's this black cloud over me.' It is a sense of dark desolation and desperate uncertainty.

Most of us measure life's happiness and our own and others' significance chiefly by the value of relationships. Through them our needs are met and our lives are given meaning and purpose. Death severs a relationship and disrupts happiness. Bereavement disrupts the most significant relationship of all.

The bereaved are indeed bereft.

Many suffer in their anxiety from physical symptoms that are

46

common in panic-situations – a dry mouth, constricted throat and chest, palpitations, difficulty in breathing, 'a heavy weight like lead in my stomach'.

C. S. Lewis begins his personal story of bereavement thus: 'No one ever told me that grief felt so like fear, . . . the same fluttering in the stomach, the same restlessness, the yawning. I keep swallowing.'[1]

Some people seem to lose their physical energy: 'I couldn't seem to do anything, just sit around and worry. "You're going grey," my son said.' Others feel they must dash around in a bustle of needless activity, restlessly trying to smother their anxious fears.

Practical problems can loom frighteningly large:
'Shall I ever be able to manage without his money?'
'Must I sell the house?'
'Whatever shall I do about the garden and his greenhouse?'
'I can't bring up two girls on my own. Mine's not mother-love. I didn't bear them.'

Childhood fears tend to return, fears of the dark, of sleeping alone, of creaking floorboards and footsteps outside the window, of going into an empty house: 'I know I'm being silly, just childish really, but I can't help it.'

The fear or uneasiness about going into an empty house is one that often lasts for years. It is frequently mentioned and seems so unreasonable to those who have felt no such anxiety while their partner was alive, even though he would not necessarily have been in. Some have bought a dog or a budgerigar, and one elderly widow told how she always left the radio on to greet her on her return.

New fears threaten, some of them quite illogical:
'I'm scared to let the boy out of my sight.'
'I'm in a dither if the door bell rings, expecting to drop dead myself.'
'It's the traffic – it seems so menacing – I can't get across the road – I just want to scream.'
'I found a spider in the bath. They're unlucky, aren't they? I wonder who's going next.'

This stress often gives rise to moodiness and irritation and a lack of self-control that in earlier years would have been normal childish reactions but now seem inappropriate and out of character. They may cause tension with the family and neighbours, and frustration and humiliation to the bereaved themselves. 'I've not shouted at anyone like that since I was at school. Whatever's come over me? I must be out of my mind.'

The bewilderment and shame at this childish behaviour sometimes leads to the fear that 'I'm going to have a breakdown' or to the question – here it is again! – 'Am I going mad?' Others who have been longer widowed will remember their own anxiety and be able to reassure and console: 'No, you're not going mad. You're frightened and lonely and sad. We know just how you feel.'

Children under the stress of bereavement-anxiety may revert to bed-wetting or to baby-talk, or start stammering, chewing their lips or biting their nails. They may become over-dependent or demand excessive affection from the surviving parent, or show any of a hundred-and-one regressive symptoms of anxiety.

They need to be encouraged to talk, to be listened to and helped to express their fears and uncertainties and to ask the questions that death has raised for them:

'Mummy, *you* aren't going to die, are you?'

'Is it cold in a grave? I wouldn't like the dark.'

'Will Daddy always know now when I'm bad?'

'What is dead?'

'Is it true they really *burnt* my Granny?'

It sometimes takes much patience to answer children's questions, but fearful imaginings may be behind them which can cause trouble even years later if they are not talked through. The last question above was asked by a 6-year-old whose grandmother's body had lately been cremated. It took patient, gentle chat to elicit that cremation – burning – was imagined to have been the *cause* of death, and that, being a granny, the babysitter was in danger of a similar fate! Questions, especially if they are asked several times, should alert adults to the danger of unpleasant misunderstandings and fantasies that need to be dispelled. Sometimes it is assumed that children are 'too young to understand'. Yes indeed, but not too young to *mis*understand.

In talking about death with children I often have the impression that they accept it almost intuitively as a natural part of life. Perhaps it is from adult reactions and conversations that their fantasies and fears derive.

Accepting the fact of death, however, does not mean that they accept personal bereavement without distress. Children who lose a parent in their infancy will experience grief and acute anxiety at the separation. They will react with infantile anger, perhaps with listless apathy or symptoms of physical pain. They will need prolonged loving handling, and some soft huggable piece of clothing or familiar object belonging to the parent who has died may help to ease their distress. Even though too young to understand, they will nevertheless be acutely sensitive to the atmosphere created by the adults around. It is very important that they are made to feel safe and loved, not least because psychologists have taught us that their responses to loss at this early age will pattern their emotional responses to it for the rest of their lives.

At every stage of childhood grief needs to be expressed; its expression may need to be encouraged, even aroused. Grief repressed in childhood is unnatural, and harmful and dangerous to health and happiness in years to come. Even in adult life childhood bereavement has been found to be the cause of mental disturbance.

Regressive behaviour, both in adults and children, is a typical reaction to the anxiety of separation. Neither the bereaved themselves nor those around them need be surprised or frightened at it.

Separation from one who is close normally brings insecurity: 'I can never settle when he goes away.' Bereavement has brought separation for all time. It upsets the stable organisation of years. In marriage a plan of life is built up round the circumstances of the partners; the basis is usually the work-pattern of one or both of them which becomes a secure framework for convenient, comfortable living.

Death destroys this stable organised pattern of life. The security of what was known is shattered and the widowed live in a present for which they have no precedent, facing a future that can be only vaguely imagined. The uncertainties, the need for new plans, perhaps for a total restructuring of their lives, has now to be undertaken without the partner on whom life's pattern has until now so largely depended. It is likely to be a very daunting prospect.

'How shall I manage? Whatever shall I do?' Questions about the future torment anxious minds and may be asked repeatedly, even rather hysterically, as though to smother the fear and feelings of helplessness that now overwhelm. These anxieties are likely to be specially acute when death has come without forewarning. There is a danger that in this crisis the bereaved will make rash decisions that they feel driven to make, rather than carefully considered plans. This is not the moment to plan ahead or take irrevocable steps about altering one's life-style, about moving house, or changing or giving up a job. Events as well as feelings need time to settle.

'Whatever shall I do?' The best answer to this urgent question is 'Nothing just yet'. The task now is to cope with the small immediate jobs – and there will probably be plenty of them – and try to rest and relax and let others share the anxieties and help look to the future. Fears become less fearful when they are confided, and others are usually quicker to distinguish the real from the irrational. The future is not so daunting when its problems and possibilities are shared.

For those who have no friendly confidant/e to turn to, seeking help from some caring organisation, counselling service or counsellor is a positive, constructive way of helping oneself.[2]

ANGER

Perhaps at first glance anger is not an emotion that seems appropriate in mourning. However, those who have made professional studies of bereavement have found it a strong component of the grieving process. Dr Elisabeth Kübler-Ross, who has spent much of her life helping the dying 'to die well' and the living to understand better the inner crisis through which the dying are passing, writes that 'the process of grief always includes elements of anger'.[3]

We would all recognise anger as a common reaction to loss, and loss is the basic element in grief.

I recall an incident unconnected with death which illustrates well this spontaneous anger-reaction in a loss situation. I found a small mentally handicapped boy wandering in the lane and recognised him as the much loved son of a friendly young couple. I took him home. Expecting profuse thanks, I was taken aback when I was met by a tearful, sullen mother and a very angry father who smacked the child and shouted threats to strangle someone unknown who must have left the gate open. The mother screamed that the dinner was spoiled, for which she appeared to blame me, and rushed inside slamming the door. Later all three came round to see us, much embarrassed and very apologetic. Their outbursts were wholly out of character. They were the sort of angry, uncontrolled reaction that loss arouses, a misdirected rage against those who did not deserve their blame. For the time of the child's absence these parents were bereft; their angry reactions showed the depth of their anxiety.

Sometimes the anger of grief is shown as a generalised irritability or bad temper or as gnawing resentment against those who are happy and unaware of tragedy, or it may well up suddenly in outraged indignation. It has many guises and chooses its own, usually inconvenient, moment to erupt.

Mary Stott writes: 'Rage creeps up on you unawares . . . as I walked along a crowded compartment and saw people laughing and talking and reading and sleeping, something in my mind went briefly out of gear. Their normality was hideous to me. I was in hostile country, an enemy alien.'[4] Many widowed people will recognise and sympathise with her feelings.

The bereaved have lost someone, perhaps the only person who gave life purpose and meaning. Their happiness is shattered and their peace of mind outraged:
'This should not have happened. It is not fair. Someone is to blame.'
'What have I done to deserve this?'
'He was a good man: why should he die when all these hooligans are about?'
'Why, why, why should this happen to me?'

Sometimes in their grief mourners show their anger against the dead, perhaps actually naming them or blaming them for having 'left us to manage on our own'. It is the anger of the forsaken against those who have abandoned them:

'He should never have gone out. I said stay in and keep warm.'
'She never would take her medicine.'
'She's left me with a fate worse than death.'
'He had no right to leave me like this. He never complained of a pain.'
'Mummy wouldn't have died if she had properly loved us'; or simply, 'Oh, John, how could you?'

But hostility towards the dead, especially one deeply loved and mourned, is not a feeling that is easily admitted by the bereaved nor accepted as appropriate by those around them, so anger is unconsciously diverted and resentment and aggression is turned on others.

Unless this misdirected anger is understood, it is very hard for those around to take. It is often fantastic and irrational; the grounds for it may be imagined or grossly exaggerated; the language will be bitterly resentful. It is the expression of the feelings of someone in the pain of grief, and although the accusations may be utterly false or distorted, the feelings and the pain and the loss are real.

Hospital staff are often the targets of this misdirected anger. Nurses have told of their distress when, after they have nursed a dying patient and had a good relationship with both the patient and the relatives, and have been gratefully thanked for their care and kindness, the relatives have returned later to complain with bitter anger over some slight or imagined mistake – the non-return of a toothbrush or perhaps a mis-spelt name.

A widow told of her bitter anger which she expressed very strongly when she was kept waiting for a death certificate 'as the post-mortem is not quite finished'. Later she felt ashamed of her rudeness and realised that her anger was caused not by the wait, for she was in fact early, but by her fantasy about what was going on while she waited.

Doctors are often blamed by the bereaved – after all, they have failed to cure and it was for that that the patients consulted them. Communication between doctor and patient, and between doctor and relative, can be very poor. The professionals are over-busy and probably more deeply affected than they care to show, and the lay people are unfamiliar with medical language and slow to understand what they do not want to hear.

Funeral directors and the clergy are other targets for anger. The clergy seem to evoke more anger than the funeral director, who is usually seen as a helpful, benevolent figure, at least until the funeral bill comes in. But the clergy are the representatives of God and He may be the one against whom bitter resentment is felt, if He is seen at this time as the Cruel Disposer rather than the Loving Father bringing release from pain and weariness. 'Don't come here talking to me about God,' a vicar was told as the door slammed in his face, 'Look what He's done to me.'

Family quarrels, of which the seeds have perhaps lain dormant for years, sometimes erupt under the strain of bereavement because the mourners' angry feelings cannot be contained and may be directed or misdirected against those they love.

There may be a difficult situation with in-laws who are, of course, also bereaved and under stress and may feel that their needs are receiving too little consideration.

Wills often cause serious disputes and divisions. Belongings suddenly assume great importance when financial security is threatened and the personal possessions of the dead sometimes become valued fetishes, enshrining something of their previous owner.

Years after her husband's death a widow told of her estrangement from her brother-in-law who had 'taken illegal possession' of her husband's bicycle, which she could never have used. After recounting the incident she looked up with a nervous smile and said: 'It was all very silly. I really must write to him.'

When anger is not expressed, it gnaws away inside and makes peace of mind impossible. It tends to break out in hostility or unwarranted resentment in unguarded moments so that relationships with family or neighbours are embittered. It is tragic when this anger smoulders on.

A widow, more than thirty years after the Second World War in which her submariner husband lost his life, still found herself 'furiously jealous' of happily married couples and, while longing for friends, alienated almost everyone by her ungracious defensiveness. Thirty years of grievous unhappiness because the anger at her loss had never been accepted or expressed and had isolated her in friendlessness!

Most adults have evolved inner mechanisms for diffusing their angry feelings and these will gradually do their work, though it is helpful when the pressures of bereavement are understood and can be recognised and worked through, if possible with those who are not themselves emotionally involved.

GUILT

There is no grave beside which a flood of guilt does not assail the mind. (PAUL TOURNIER)

A small boy was found sobbing on his first day back at school because 'I didn't say goodbye to my donkey and he will never, never forgive me.'

In most separations, even temporary ones, there is often a guilty feeling that we have not done everything we should have done for the one who is away. The separation in bereavement is permanent, and remorse – the gnawing pain of conscience – is intensified because it is felt that there is now nothing that can be done about it, no way of 'putting things right' and he can 'never, never forgive me'. It seems then quite impossible to forgive oneself, and the result is a bitter, guilty anxiety that is a frequent, if not universal, element in grief.

Guilt is a matter of fact, but guilty feelings may be and often are quite unrealistic. It is, for peace of mind, well worth trying to distinguish the one from the other.

Imagined guilt about a death may cause much unnecessary misery to children who hide in the dark corners of their consciousness fears which they do not readily reveal:

'I'll kill you,' they may have shouted in a rage; is that why he's dead?

'You'll make Mummy ill if you scream like that'; so it's my fault!

'Granny often said I would be the death of her'; whatever did I do?

54

'I hate my sister. I wish she'd drop down dead'; now she is in hospital – is she going to die?

A lad of fifteen had a violent argument with his parents and went off to spend the night with a friend. The parents, setting off to look for him, drove out of the garage into the path of a speeding lorry and were both killed. It was only when he was at college five years later and nearly had a serious breakdown that he uncovered his guilty belief that he had caused his parents' death.

There is often a vague disquiet that something could have been done to alter the course of events:

'Where did I go wrong?'

'What more could I have done?'

'I'm sure he wasn't meant to die.'

'If only I had . . .'

'If only, if only . . .' – unhappy, guilt-ridden words, but rarely with any factual foundation.

Sometimes the bereaved are full of remorse that they were not present at the time of death, as if they had failed the dying at the last and had 'missed the chance to say goodbye': 'It's the last thing I could have done for him.'

In cases of long illness there may be wishes, secret or expressed, that 'this agony won't go on much longer' or feelings of relief that 'at last it's all over'. These very natural feelings cause much guilty concern, and those who are able to admit to them are astonished to find that others are not shocked; they too may have had just such thoughts. They are the product of the anxiety of separation, and when they are consciously acknowledged and talked through, they cease to be a guilty problem.

Many blame themselves for something concerned with the last illness and regret what they did or did not do:

'I ought to have fetched the doctor sooner.'

'I should have stopped him smoking.'

'I could have defied the hospital. She wanted to come home.'

'She said she'd like a budgie for her birthday, and I said I'd get her one next year.'

Then there are the self-accusing torments of those who do not feel or behave as they think is expected of those who mourn:

'It isn't that I don't care, but I can't cry. Well, you can't just turn the tap on.'

'I find I forget about him – and when I remember it seems too bad of me to forget so soon.'

'I keep thinking I'll get married again, but I know that's disloyal of me.'

'I don't like to say it and I do miss him, but I'm glad to be on my own again.'

And some feel guilty because 'in a tied-up way, I'm glad I'm alive. It seems wrong when she's gone and I loved her.'

This feeling of guilt about being the one to remain alive is so common amongst the bereaved that psychiatrists have coined a phrase for it. They call it 'survivor guilt'. It is especially likely to be felt by those who survive some incident in which others died, as in a car crash, a multiple accident or in war.

Others are concerned and often bitterly distressed at their failures or shortcomings in the marriage:

'I could have been a better wife to him' (who couldn't say that with truth?).

'I didn't always treat her right, not gently and all that.'

There may be guilty memories of a past – perhaps long past – infidelity or some guilty secret it is now too late to share.

Those who are around the bereaved too often try to console them in their remorse by such advice as: 'Don't carry on like that; you've nothing to blame yourself for.' This is a natural reaction, kindly and well-meant, but it is unlikely to be true. There are very, very few perfect marriages, or relationships – very, very few spouses who have 'nothing to blame themselves for'. Perhaps it is better to learn to accept our partners' imperfections and our own failings, and remember the relationship as it really was, letting the truth set us free to love and remember without remorse the real person whom we have lost.

For some the burden of guilt is so great that it is not brought into full consciousness, and then unconsciously they try to compensate for it and make reparation. They may overspend on an expensive funeral as though to convince themselves and others of their partner's worth and their great love; or they may put him on a pedestal, over-praising and idealising him, perhaps almost convincing even themselves of his outstanding virtues; or they may be unable to stop grieving, as though to make reparation through continued painful grief.

As with children, so with adults; the burden of guilt needs to be shared. Though this is no longer possible with the one who has been wronged, the very speaking of guilt out loud brings relief.

Ministers of religion and those who share a Christian faith will be able to affirm and assure that the gospel of forgiveness makes continued guilt wholly out of place; 'No one need continue to feel guilty before God unless he chooses to . . . there is nothing that cannot be forgiven except the refusal to accept forgiveness.'[5]

A wise counsellor will accept what is said, trying perhaps to do away with any superstition or fallacies, but not denying the wrong nor apportioning blame. It is a sign of trust and acceptance when someone is able to reveal deep and guilty feelings, and a most moving, healing experience to find one's shame and guilt accepted with warm-hearted understanding.

With time and understanding help and returning confidence most will be able to come to terms with their regrets, distinguishing the imagined from the real guilt and letting sorrow dwell only where it truly belongs.

1. C. S. Lewis, *A Grief Observed*, p. 7.
2. Sources of advice and help for the bereaved can be found in the Appendix.
3. Elisabeth Kübler-Ross, *On Death and Dying*, Tavistock Publications, 1970.
4. *Forgetting's No Excuse*, p. 183.
5. Ruth Fowkes, *Coping with Crises* (Hodder and Stoughton), p. 78.

Reminiscence

I remember, I remember. (THOMAS HOOD)

During the yearning stage of grief the bereaved are beginning to realise that the dead are no longer an immediate and present part of their lives, and are slowly and reluctantly learning to disengage their thoughts and habits from the dead person's live presence. One of the ways in which they gradually break the ties that bind them to the past is reminiscence.

But these ties are strong and the process of breaking them sometimes has about it a nightmarish quality:
'My mind won't shut up. I wish it would leave me alone.'
'My head is a whirling inferno and I can't escape.'
There is a sense of compulsion to talk and unload the weight of jumbled thoughts and memories in an endless repetition. This sort of reminiscence is a relief to some, though probably something of a burden to those around.

A more gentle form of reminiscence is that of recounting over and over again the details of the last illness, the funeral and visits of family and friends. Mourners will tell of their last Christmas or holiday with the one who has died or describe some event which they enjoyed together. Almost anything will awaken memories, perhaps a radio programme: 'He always loved those two, never missed them'; or a chance remark about the weather: 'Your Dad would have been in the garden on a day like this.'

Often they will speak in the present tense, forgetting for the moment that the one who was so much a part of their lives is not with them any more: 'We always go to Eastbourne and I watch him playing bowls . . . well, I mean, that's how it used to be.' They may be embarrassed or tearful at this slip of the tongue – more accurately, a slip of the memory – but the very embarrassment is a reminder of the truth.

It is easy for the family to lose patience with this endless repetition:
'Oh, Mum, we've heard it all before – besides, we were there.'
'Don't keep reminding yourself of what's past, dear.'
Members of the family have their own need to adjust to the death in their own way and may well find this seemingly useless prattle very irritating, but it is a natural beneficial activity, a safety-valve or a comforting, gentle expedient by which, while keeping less and less hold on their dead, the living gradually learn to let them go.

Generally the process of reminiscing works backwards. Just as the elderly tend to recall events further and further in the past as they grow older, so those who are grieving usually dwell first on the last days and weeks, the funeral and the family gathering, the death and the illness and the details of its onset and then perhaps of the last holiday or Christmas and back and back over the years together. As their reminiscences come from further and further in the past, they are gradually, unconsciously, effortlessly letting their loved ones go from their immediate present experience while keeping them alive in their memories and hearts.

Reminiscing has another positive value; it helps the widowed to explore the meaning of the marriage relationship and to discover what remains after the bodily presence has gone. As the ties that bind the living to the dead are loosened, pondering on memories, character, personal eccentricities and characteristics, shared happiness and sorrow, establishes the personality of the one who has died as it was truly in life. From this there can grow the realisation that what *was* true *is* true now. The essence and deep meaning of the relationship has not changed and can remain for the living as a real part of what they possess and what they are. Gradually this sense of continuity helps towards acceptance of their situation.

Reminiscing may turn to brooding if it has no audience: 'I'm afraid of forgetting.' But it is not every friend or neighbour who can resist the temptation to intervene, who will not only listen but will encourage the flow of memories and allow tears to come freely. Talking and crying are natural ways of expressing feelings of pain, and the deep pain of grief needs to be expressed. Repressed it is damaging to body and mind, but expressed it has a healing quality. And reminiscence recalls happiness as well as sorrow. It revives the joys and delights and quiet contentment which will be remembered with love and gently savoured and stored away to bring much comfort in days to come. It brings pleasure as well as relief.

Many of those who are suffering years after the bereavement because grief was repressed or suppressed and recovery has been long delayed, are suffering simply because there was no one at hand ready to listen when they needed to remember and speak of the joys and sorrows of the past. I have no doubt whatever that the most valuable support in the early months of bereavement is given by a good listener, especially one who is not too closely involved with the family's emotional distress.

Depression

The valley of the shadow . . . (PSALM 23)

Depression is a word that is loosely used and ill-defined. It is not used here in any technical psychological sense, but as a general description of the mood that is ordinarily understood by such phrases as 'I feel so depressed' or 'What a depressing sort of day'. It is a natural inevitable reaction to loss, and those who are bereaved will not escape it.

The stage of yearning, with its intensity of feeling and emotional disturbance, passes gradually into depression. Emotions and behaviour do not change suddenly; one cannot say, as with chickenpox, that today the rash has gone. Most of the acute symptoms of loss already described – anxiety, anger, guilt, particularly guilt – will overwhelm from time to time, but in a way that is now more passive than active, in which it is less of an effort to give in and endure than to react. It is as though passions and overwrought senses can no longer keep going, but are insisting on a period of retrenchment. This depression is a natural reaction to over-stimulated emotions, a much needed period of emotional convalescence.

The chief mark of this depressive mood is apathy, a lack of excitement and intensity of feeling, wanting in initiative, self-reliance, self-esteem, self-respect and even self-interest, and with strong temptations to self-pity. Those who are depressed will probably eat without enjoyment, sleep without feeling rested and complain that they are not well without being able to describe their symptoms or locate the pain. It is a time of great poverty of spirit, of dejection and grey bleakness that for

61

some amounts to almost hopeless despair and for others is a joyless monotony of emptiness and lethargy.

Other people's enjoyment of life is an intrusion and their impatient advice to 'pull yourself together', 'snap out of it', 'stop thinking about your troubles' increases the sense of isolation, for it seems that these others just do not understand. Those who do understand stay nearby and give support, realising that to be sad and depressed is natural to those who are striving to cope with shock and anger and guilt and learning to accept their loss.

A widow, bereaved for several months, said: 'It's all hurt and hurt. Why on earth do I go on?' This question is often asked in one form or another by those who feel the struggle is going against them:

'I'm at the end of my tether.'

'I think I'm going to have a nervous breakdown; it feels like breaking down.'

'I'm too tired to bother to cope any more.'

Many have said or thought:

'I wish I were dead' or 'I wouldn't mind if I could join him'.

'This just isn't my idea of life; what's it all for?'

And they have said it without any desire or intention to bring life to an end.

A psychiatrist wrote: 'When questioned sympathetically many people will reluctantly admit that they feel it is no longer worth the struggle to go on living. They are usually quite honest in their assessment of whether or not they are likely to harm themselves.'[1]

The majority – the vast majority – of the bereaved do not seriously contemplate suicide which is the act of someone who is sick, suffering from the kind of depression that is an illness, but it would be wrong to ignore the possibility that someone in a period of depression might be seriously ill and needing psychiatric help. 'The belief that people who talk about suicide never attempt it is quite without foundation. On the contrary, it is usual for them to give some warning of their desperate plight.'[2] It would be a matter for direct reference to their GP, or an immediate call for help to the Samaritans.[3]

A widower told how he 'just didn't want to go on living' until he remembered that his daughter was pregnant. He cried as he told of his wife's unfulfilled longing to live to see the baby and of his own deep desire to hold his grandchild and watch it grow up. There was a responsive stir of sympathy and understanding amongst those who heard this and who in spite of their own yearning and distress were able to support him.

It is so often the hope of continuing life and love in children and grandchildren that brings comfort and courage to the widowed. Children are often kept away from sadness and excluded from visits to the dying and the bereaved, but sadness is a part of life's make-up and can be a positive developing experience, especially when the sad are made glad in the love they receive and give.

The stage of depression usually occurs when mourning is almost completed, so there is some encouragement to be found even in this unpleasant time. It *is* a wretched time, but a hopeful one because it precedes and presages recovery.

There are many books about depression, best read probably when one is not in its throes. I know of one, however, that has proved very helpful to many in bereavement, even while they have been suffering from its inevitable depressive miseries. It is small, cheap and easy to read. It was written by a Christian psychotherapist who knows personally what she has written about. It is full of good sense and sympathetic understanding. Even its title, 'Coping with Depression', wastes no words.[4]

I turn now to some particular aspects of the normal depressive stage of grief.

LOSS OF IDENTITY

'I can't explain myself' . . . *said Alice, 'because I'm not myself.'*
(LEWIS CARROLL)

The sense of a loss of identity as a result of bereavement is almost exclusively confined to widows, who are generally identified and identify themselves with the husbands whose names they have taken. We speak of the Mayor's Lady, the doctor's wife, but after his death, although she keeps his name, she is no longer his wife.

The widow is therefore especially vulnerable to a feeling of nonentity, to a loss of personal significance and to uncertainty about her social role. She tends to reckon herself negatively as a no-longer-what-I-was person. She may sometimes find herself described on old tombstones or in current legal documents as the 'relict' of So-and-So, a term that – I am assured by a professor of law – is never used of husbands.

She is half, and feels less than half, of a broken partnership, like the child who on her first day at school was asked her name: 'I'm Ann,' she said, 'all that's left of twins.'

Two widows were helping at a jumble sale, and one held up an old shopping bag and asked what was in it. 'Oh, just remnants,' she was told. She turned to her companion with a wry smile: 'Just remnants! Like us, dear.'

All that's left, relicts, remnants, things left behind! Consciously or unconsciously this is how many widows value themselves and how society often regards them. They are survivors of something now past with no present assured position in the community. The no-longer-what-I-was person now asks herself: 'Who am I?'

The widow of a doctor, answering the telephone some weeks after her husband's death, said: 'Doctor Blank's house – his wife speaking.' Then inadvertently she dropped the phone. When she picked it up the line was dead. She found that she was shaking and feeling rather sick and sat down to steady herself. 'I am not Doctor Blank's wife,' she thought, 'Who am I?' As she told of this incident to a group of widowed people, the women shared her embarrassment and sense of confused identity: What should she have said? Who was she now? Who were they?

Separated from the one perhaps casually called in the past 'my better half', the survivor must now establish a single identity and seek an individual independence that she does not yet want, one that is valid for herself, her family and friends, and for society. For the most part society does little to help in this process of re-establishment.

LOSS OF SOCIAL STATUS

The social status of a widow is clearly different from that of a married woman: in Western society it is tacitly considered inferior.

Widows often find that their income is reduced, and this is likely to affect their social life. It may mean that they must move to a smaller house or resign from clubs and organisations, or give up the kind of holidays and entertaining that they have been accustomed to. They will no longer be invited to functions which they attended as their husbands' wives and will be excluded from social activities arranged for couples. Widowers too may now have less money and more commitments if they have to pay for the care of the children and house, or give up work to do this themselves, and they may be the poorer by the loss of the wife's wage.

The usual pattern of entertaining which is so often organised for pairs seems fortunately to be breaking down, especially among the young who do not accept the need for this formality. The tradition that a dining-table must seat pairs of opposite sex often means that the widow is out of place, or in a less formal gathering she may find herself the odd-one-out, the 'fifth wheel' as Americans call her.

Many women hesitate to accept invitations from men and are equally hesitant to spend evenings alone in public, feeling out of place in a public-house and conspicuous even in a restaurant. They therefore spend their leisure hours alone or with other women who are on their own. Most now have fewer male contacts as they tend to drift away from those who were primarily their husbands' friends and colleagues, though women who have jobs may be less affected as their colleagues and work-status will perhaps provide some social opportunities.

Among young widows an ambivalence about identity or status sometimes surfaces in discussion as a problem about wearing a wedding-ring. If they wear it they may seem to be 'not available', yet to abandon it leaves them feeling 'stateless' or 'disloyal': 'It seems to leave me nowhere'; 'It's a bit of a lie either way.'

They complain too that they are regarded as a threat by their married friends, who ask them to coffee or an evening meal only when husbands are out. Some find they no longer share the interests of couples, since their status and income are reduced, and they are not as socially acceptable as they used to be.

Widowers too are seen as threats to established marriages and may therefore find themselves socially less acceptable.

It is difficult for the shy widow or widower to have a satisfying social life, as this generally means making new contacts at a time of particular sensitivity, but there are possible ways of making new friendships that are not too threatening: by joining evening classes or a choir, where others will be enjoying the same activity; by getting in touch with organisations for the widowed or single parents – a phone call to the organiser (whose address will be available in the public library) will generally ensure that the new arrival is immediately welcomed; the widowed with children will be able to meet other parents at school functions or just while waiting to collect the children after school, and most churches and chapels really welcome newcomers and provide opportunities for making friends.

After the early months of bereavement the widowed who feel able to play a part in the community have many opportunities in voluntary social and charitable work, or in organisations in which their particular experience may be specially appreciated. There is real need and wide scope for those who are anxious to be of service.

STIGMA

We do not burn our widows, we pity and avoid them. (C. MURRAY PARKES)

There are not many people who would deliberately hurt friends, friends who are already unhappy, and yet it is a common experience for the bereaved to be avoided by those they know quite well and by whom they would previously have been greeted:
'I thought she might cry.'
'It might have upset him.'

'She could have been so embarrassed.'
'I didn't know what to say.'
Cry? Well, why not? She has something to cry about. Upset? Embarrassed? Perhaps, but the bereaved would rather be upset or embarrassed than ignored.

'I'm aware of being an embarrassment to everyone I meet . . . I see people, as they approach me, trying to make up their minds whether they'll "say something about it" or not . . . To some I'm worse than an embarrassment. I am a death's head.'[5]

Our society fears death and tries to deny its presence. Death has come very close to the bereaved and when they are around it can no longer be denied, so they must be avoided. A speaker in a radio programme spoke of them as 'having the smell of death about them'. I recoil from the phrase, but I know just what it means, and how much the bereaved suffer from this attitude.

The only defence – if defence there must be – of society's attitude is that people are largely unaware of their own deep fears and the defences they use to cover them. They fool themselves, however, if they believe that it is the bereaved whose embarrassment they are trying to save.

Surely better than defence is understanding and the recognition that those who are grieving for one they love need the love and caring kindness of their friends. It *is* difficult to know what to say, and it is embarrassing if she cries – especially if *he* cries – but it would be an act of positive friendliness to make an approach, saying perhaps very little as long as it is genuine, 'said from the heart', and giving a gentle touch. Accepting the possible tears and consequent embarrassment would be a small price to pay for the warmth, relief and gratitude that it would probably bring. Even 'Hallo' and a wave would be kinder than escape.

I have heard of an area in Ireland where the accepted behaviour on meeting one who is mourning is to shake her right hand with the left hand while holding her left upper or fore-arm with the right hand. Nothing need be said nor is it expected.

Touch can often convey more sympathy than words. Especially when given with a loving direct look, this gentle courtesy will surely be a very warming experience for one in lonely distress, and it is so simple and unaffected a gesture that it is not likely to cause embarrassment to mourner or friend.

SEXUAL DEPRIVATION

In the early days of bereavement the numbness and anxiety and weariness tend to depress and sometimes obliterate sexual desire. Sex is an instinctual affirmation of life, but it is with death that the bereaved are now chiefly involved.

Nevertheless, despite the reticence which inhibits much public discussion of this subject, it is clear that sexual deprivation presents a very real problem for most who are widowed after the first few weeks or months and before that for some. This seems to be especially, but not exclusively, true for those widowed when they are young, in their twenties, thirties and forties. It may also be true for others, but older women are hesitant, often ashamed, to admit to sexual feelings. Discussion reveals that a considerable proportion of older women miss this side of their marriage relationship in varying degrees, though not with the immediate need and urgency of the young. Most men – I am led to believe – have strong sexual desires even in the early days of bereavement.

To some the thought of another sexual relationship seems a guilty unfaithfulness, a betrayal of the one who has died, and even to indulge the thought causes anxiety and tension.

For some, the fact of being wanted by someone again and of being able to give and to get sexual satisfaction and pleasure restores a sense of significance and relieves physical tension.

Others again miss the pleasure and comfort of sex, but value it only as part of a total commitment and find the idea of sex outside marriage wholly unacceptable.

Among men, masturbation is more freely talked about than it is among women. While men speak of 'a return to masturbation as the only possible relief', women seem more hesitant, though it may be that this is chiefly a hesitancy to talk about it. Some who would welcome the relief of sexual tension find it no help, though a number of both men and women find 'it relieves great tension' and 'is an aid to sleep'.

Among young widows some complain that they feel threatened as they find themselves the objects of advances from men, sometimes the husbands of their friends, and say that they need to be careful in accepting invitations as 'sex is often the expected payment for an evening out'. Widowers too are embarrassed by the fact or the suspicion that women 'are after them' or 'find them fair game'.

Most widows miss male companionship and would welcome it:

'I'm not asking to go all the way, just to get with them and have a man's arms around me sometimes.'

'I do miss their deep voices – and their jokes.'

'Women don't admire each other and men used to make me feel great.'

'Men I used to hug avoid it now.'

Many widows feel too insecure to issue social invitations or join male company. Some are anxiously looking for remarriage, but statistics suggest that their chances are small. Some 60 per cent of widowers marry again, but the figure for widows is only about 30 per cent.

How the widowed cope with their sexual desires is a personal ethical decision. It will depend not only on the significance that their marriage gave to sexual experience but on attitudes that began to take shape in childhood and adolescence, on social and family pressures and on moral and religious convictions. It is a personal and private area of decision-making, but there are three cautions which experience suggests should be given.

1. A widow may legally be deprived of her statutory pension and some welfare rights if she is found to be cohabiting. There is no decisive legal definition of 'cohabiting', and it seems that sometimes she is not given the benefit of doubt.

2. Remarriage is unlikely to work out well if it is undertaken on the rebound, before the grief of the previous bereavement has been satisfactorily worked through and the ties with the first partner loosened – though they are not likely to be unremembered. However strong the sexual attraction and desire it is not *in itself* a sufficient basis for remarriage;

other aspects of the relationship need to be considered if the new partnership is to survive.

3. A new marriage commitment is not likely to last unless the one who is widowed is reconciled to the loss and is not looking for a repetition of the earlier marriage, and the other recognises that the bereaved cannot deny or depreciate the first love. Remarriage is a new, uncharted adventure and likely to have more hazards than the first one.[6]

LOSS OF RELIGIOUS FAITH

Where is God? (C. S. LEWIS)

What follows refers only to those who affirm a Christian belief, who would call themselves non-churchgoing Christians or committed Christians or something in between. Regretfully I have no experience of this aspect of grief among those of other faiths.

It would be more accurate to speak of disturbance, rather than loss of faith, since doubts and questionings will generally take the form of an angry reaction or a bewildered cry of distress rather than a considered rejection of accepted belief. 'Meanwhile, where is God?' wrote C. S. Lewis,[7] a deeply religious thinker who became a Christian after years of agnosticism and searching.

It is a deeply disturbing – and not a rare experience – for Christians to find it impossible to reconcile God's apparent injustice or lack of concern towards them with the concept of the loving Father in whom they have hitherto trusted:
'I am very angry with God, very angry,' a widow repeated fiercely, too distressed to reason, but very sure her tragedy was His fault.
'I never thought He would leave me in the lurch just when I really wanted Him.'
'It's God's cruelty I'm wrestling with.'
    Prayer may become seemingly irrelevant:
'It can't bring her back.'
'What chokes every prayer . . . is the memory of all the prayers [we] offered.'[8]

'He doesn't seem to be listening, whatever the Bible says.'

Church-going may evoke memories so that tears cannot be controlled:
'It takes me back to our wedding.'
'I just find myself crying like at Mum's funeral.'
It is easier, less embarrassing to stay away.

Some give up church-going for reasons that they do not understand and find only mildly disturbing and 'there's always the radio'. Perhaps they are unconsciously unsatisfied with answers to questions of belief which did not disturb them in the past: 'It all seems a bit irrelevant now.'

Many people for whom religion has had little or no significance ('We aren't religious; we like Christmas and all that for the children') may now find themselves asking heart-searching questions, though probably without expecting to find answers:
'I wish someone would explain where she is.'
'I don't see how "gone to Jesus" makes him happy.'
'I'd like to believe he's somewhere.'
'We can't *know* anything, can we? But I do wonder.'
'Why did God take him and leave the prisons full?'
'Why should this happen to *me*?'
That's the really nagging question: Why me? Why him? Why her? Why?

In spite of the comforting words of the funeral service and the tenuous belief in a loving God revived from childhood, there now sounds a note of fear, fear of the loneliness and loveless-ness of what is left of life, fear of one's own death, fear that nothing, no one can be relied on. How can God fail us like this if He is really there?

I believe that it is somewhere here that faith seems to be lost, for who would consciously assert that God was lacking in love? Even in the most secret places of their hearts few would dare to affirm that God was bad, for that surely is the final blasphemy. It is safer, certainly less terrible, not to believe in Him at all. So:
'I lost my faith when she was taken.'
'I can't believe in that any more. Lots don't. I think that's sensible.'

'I don't want a God who could let him suffer like he did.'
'Where is God in all this? May be, nowhere.'

Only very rarely, I have come to believe, do these disturbing questions call for a theological answer, at least in the early days of bereavement distress. In the wake of death there is so often a terrifying, shattering collapse of the whole structure of the life that has been built up over the years; the very foundations are shaken. It is this seemingly utter destruction of all that has been taken for granted, all that we have come to expect, that undermines faith and makes hearts cry out in angry helplessness.

Whatever beliefs or practice of religion the bereaved may have had in the past, doubts and distrust are familiar symptoms of bereavement depression. They do not generally seem to be permanently burdensome. As the anger of grief subsides there is no longer any need to seek a target for it, and it then becomes possible to renew an earlier relationship with the One whom they worshipped. It is perhaps that, like children, once their anger is spent they return to a parent with confidence.

Some will tell how they found that they 'turned back to God in spite of themselves', perhaps as they discovered within their slowly returning equanimity some reasons for thankfulness and hope.

C. S. Lewis asked, 'Where is God?', but not long afterwards he wrote: 'Turned to God I no longer meet a locked door' and 'by praising I can in some degree enjoy Him.'[9]

Or might it be that the God whom one expected would protect against such a tragedy is infinitely greater than a meagre, puerile faith has yet grasped – that a deeper faith, a less vulnerable dependency and a more profound relationship are now available to those who have lived with sorrow and are acquainted with grief?

Men and women whose faith has been tested in crises of their own can be very helpful at this time if they share and explore rather than preach. Christian ministers will be able to strengthen and undergird returning faith with the gospel of One who through suffering and death brought a new dimension of life to His friends.

1. and 2. Ruth Fowkes, *Coping with Crises*, p. 52.
3. See Appendix.
4. Myra Chave-Jones, *Coping with Depression*. Lion Publishing, 1971.
5. C. S. Lewis, *A Grief Observed*, p. 12.
6. A recent report in Marriage Guidance, published by the National Marriage Guidance Council, states that 40% of second marriages end in divorce.
7. C. S. Lewis, *A Grief Observed*, p. 9.
8. *Ibid.*, p. 26.
9. *Ibid.*, p. 49.

Loneliness

I dread loneliness but I revel in solitude. (R. S.)

Loneliness is part of every stage of grief. For many, if not for most, 'it's with us for keeps'. It is not confined to the bereaved, but it is the most intractable and enduring problem of widowhood. So many today are living away from other members of their families, perhaps in high-rise flats or on estates where those living there have not known each other long. The elderly will, in the nature of things, have lost old friends and contemporaries, and infirmity and financial stringency make visiting difficult.

A general widespread sense of isolation is greatly aggravated for the widowed. Life's values are determined and given meaning through personal relationships. To lose a close relationship of love is to suffer an isolation and loneliness in the whole of one's personality. It is loss of a part of the way in which one knows and values oneself. It affects not only what we feel, but what we do and what we are.

Loneliness results also from the normal reactions to the loss: numbness sets the widowed apart; searching brings no reward; anger alienates; guilt humiliates; depression is unattractive and makes others impatient; the stigma of widowhood erects a barrier which separates.

And loneliness tends to be self-propagating because it is often inward-looking and bolsters self-pity, which may drive others away. And the essence of loneliness – obvious, yes, but nonetheless relevant – is that it has to be borne alone.

There is physical loneliness. He is missing or she has gone; there just is no one there. There is no voice, no footstep, no loving touch nor familiar face. One chair is empty and so is one half of the bed.

'There's just emptiness.'

'I used to hate his messy gumboots in my kitchen; now I'd welcome them.'

'I just ache for her smile when I go into the empty house.'

There is social loneliness: no one to go out with or cook a meal for; no one to please or tease; 'No point in making myself look nice these days.' Walks and meals are solitary, evenings long and tedious. Weekends? 'I just dread them.'

'Sunday is the worst day. When we first retired we said, "Every day is like Sunday – it's such a happy day." We agreed that if we had ten years of this, we'd be quite prepared for it to be all over. We had just three years of it. And so Sundays become dreadfully lonely, miserable days.'

Holidays too may have lost their excitement; they are avoided or tolerated, rarely any longer carefully planned and budgeted for and anticipated with pleasure:

'I could bear to be alone if it wasn't for all the others with their partners.'

'I'm no good at going back to places where we had fun together.'

'I don't go away, it's better here where we were most together.'

It might be that talking about holidays with a friend or in a group would bring a lonely widow her first small thrill of excitement, a tiny breakthrough from her loneliness. If so, please don't let the thrill be swamped; pick it up! There are holidays specially arranged for those who are on their own, and it might be that in a group there would be less chance of loneliness. It is possible to find opportunities for holidays that are not lonely. Many suggestions are given in a holiday list published by Cruse (see Appendix).

The bitterest loneliness of all is, I believe, that which comes from the loss of shared experience: 'Now there is only me and mine where once was us and ours. Perhaps there's a rainbow or a lovely sunset, a superb concert or a challenging radio programme – they are seen and heard alone. An unexpected bill, a marriage problem in the family, a leaking roof or a car accident, whatever the trouble it can no longer be shared with the one we would wish to share it with.

Even a 'Pools' win loses its savour: 'My! *We* could have done with it! But when it came, I gave the cheque away.'

The young widowed parent has to carry alone the responsibility for bringing up a family, without the consolation of sharing the problems or the joy of relishing together the moments of success and happiness. In a short film of a young widow bringing up two small children there is a moment when the younger child takes his first step. The mother longs to share her excitement, but with whom? For most of those who viewed it, this moment was almost unbearably poignant.

For the elderly, loneliness is often a grievous burden. It is sad, though seemingly inevitable with the present economic work structure, that death so often intervenes just when a couple are planning or have started to enjoy retirement. One or both may have borne a heavy workload over the years and they will have looked forward, saved and planned for a time of more leisure and more opportunity to share its enjoyment.

Some couples may have moved house, perhaps fulfilling a dream of a country bungalow with a garden; when one partner dies the other will be in a strange place, maybe with a garden she does not want and away from old friends and a well-known neighbourhood. Like the 75-year old widow quoted earlier who 'had just three years of it', others too will find their days 'dreadfully lonely'.

This all seems to augur a bleak time ahead. Sadly, for some it may be so. But there are many bereaved people who have surmounted the bitterness of being alone, and some who have found rich opportunities in new activities and friendships. Although there is still much to be done in neighbourliness and the provision of help for the bereaved, it is possible in most areas in this country to find an organisation or social group that is wanting to know and care for those who are lonely.

For some, loneliness, a-lone-ness, may be the opportunity to experience the quiet joy that can be found only in solitude. There are productive activities that can only be practised on one's own. Some have learnt to play an instrument, which

76

might have been an excruciating experience for a marriage partner! Others have passed time catching up on reading and have found it far more enjoyable now that they can read in depth and at leisure rather than in spare minutes snatched from a busy day. Some have learnt a foreign language, perhaps through radio lessons, while others have used the media to indulge a new or revived interest in astronomy, heraldry, politics or one of a hundred other possible subjects. A number – perhaps a rather surprisingly large number – have turned their minds to meditation.

Two kinds of activity seem particularly to encourage healing of the spirit.

The first is any form of creativity. Striving to bring something original into being is a positive personal assertion that life is, after all, worthwhile. Even small creative achievement is balm to those who are weary of the pain of loss and death.

Some have taken up painting or pottery, embroidery, weaving, woodcarving, perhaps going to classes for the first time since they left school. Others have tried their skill with words, writing stories or articles, poetry, a novel or autobiography; they may have joined a local writers' circle where they will have found advice and encouragement. A widower found consolation in writing to his daughter in Australia and was surprised and delighted to discover that he was regularly contributing to a 'Letter from Home' series in a local Queensland magazine, and many of the verses and messages now found in greeting cards were written by a widow to fill lonely hours. Those who are adventurous may find they can add something to their income, but even more valuable is their sense of achievement which brings new-found zest for living. Many lonely people have shared the experience of Robert Bridges who wrote:

I too will something make
And joy in the making.[1]

Another sphere of activity, gentle or strenuous as one may choose, which seems to have a special healing quality, is one that brings us in touch with nature: country walks, fishing, gardening, collecting shells or pebbles along a quiet stretch of beach, propagating and caring for house-plants or a herb garden – the opportunities are many and varied. In the closeness to natural and living things – sun, sea, rain and wind, earth and seeds and grass, woods, trees and flowers, birds and butterflies – in the sight and sound and feel of natural elements and growing things, many have found themselves refreshed and at peace.

It is a hopeful, gladdening experience to listen to those who are still rather sad at heart telling of their hobbies, and sharing the quiet joy and precious contentment that they have found in productive solitude.

1. Robert Bridges, 'I Love All Beauteous Things'.

Acceptance

I have discovered that tragedy need not diminish those who suffer it. (CHRISTOPHER LEACH)

'Time is a great healer' the bereaved are often told, a truism in which they find little comfort since it is usually offered in the early days when healing is not what mourners are concerned with. And there seems within it a vague inference that what is needed is to wait in meek resignation while time passes. The fact is that grieving is a hard painful process that demands positive courage and patience.

For most people the loss does become more bearable, the grief less acute as time goes by, but this is due not so much to the passage of time as to what time holds, the daily insistent reminders that things are not as they were, that circumstances have changed, that established expectations, habitual ways of behaving and thinking are no longer appropriate.

The bereaved gradually find that they have rearranged their daily lives to suit themselves; they have evolved a new pattern for their day. They choose the TV and radio programmes that they like best, cater for their own tastes and do things for themselves that they would not have undertaken in the past.

A widow told how, when a door fell off a cupboard, she went to telephone for a handyman, but before she rang she wondered if perhaps she could do it herself. She was 'no use with tools' but she managed it. 'And wasn't I pleased with myself! Really pleased I felt, first time for weeks.'

Another almost sold her husband's car to a prospective buyer who said, 'Why don't you learn to drive it yourself?' She did, and found 'an independence I had never dreamed of'.

As the pattern of life changes and new opportunities present themselves, the past imperceptibly loses its hold. It becomes past. A new present is accepted, a new future is glimpsed ahead. But the past is not forgotten. It is important for the present and the future that it should *not* be forgotten.

A widow who had been very seriously injured in a car crash in which her husband was killed and a child badly injured, was given this advice when she recovered consciousness: 'Try to forget it, dear. Just think of the future. You'll soon get over it.' It may seem kindly, sensible advice to those who have not known tragedy, but months later this young woman told of it obsessively. She was much more upset about the advice than about the appalling accident and her own injuries: 'I don't want to forget; I'm still trying to remember. I'll never get over it. I just want him back.' Those who have themselves been widowed in traumatic circumstances will sympathise with her anger and frustration. 'Think of the future!' – the future did not bear thinking about. 'Forget. Get over it' – and so, she felt, let go of the little she had left?

This widow was able to share her experience with a small group of bereaved men and women, some of whom had come to accept and live at peace with the fact of their loss. The discussion that followed her account of the accident and its aftermath was honest, courageous, gentle and full of simple spontaneous wisdom.

No one liked the phrase 'getting over it' because it seemed to play down a devastating experience, to belittle the awesomeness of death, to undervalue the person who had died and make light of his widow's grief. 'Forget it', they were agreed, was bad advice and in any case quite impossible. Forgetting was negative and destructive. It had no part in healing.

'It's when you remember and it hurts that you know it really happened. That's when you begin to get better.'

'Let it hurt you, dear, pain isn't always bad.'

As the other members of the group recalled the circumstances of their own bereavements, in spite of some tears and obvious distress, it became clear that the very re-telling was a comforting experience, that sharing their feelings helped them to understand how they really felt underneath the mask that some found a necessary defence in public.

The group picked up the idea of 'getting better', a far more positive concept than 'getting over it'. They stopped mentioning the hurt of remembering and found themselves talking of their dead in the past tense, without embarrassment and even with gentle humour:

'She did like her drop of bitter!'

'I used to forget he was gone and start reading a bit out loud out of the paper; now I just think how he'd have laughed about it.'

Then someone said: 'I woke up one morning and *of course* he wasn't there, but I didn't feel badly, just lay and thought about him.' Death, though still recalled with sorrow, was no longer an appalling tragedy. '*Of course*', she said, 'of course he wasn't there.' So she affirmed, without conscious intention but quite clearly, her acceptance of the truth.

This woman's simple spontaneous remark illustrates the natural process of acceptance: 'He wasn't there. I didn't feel badly. Just lay and thought about him.'

The finality of death, the fact that the one lost cannot be recovered is recognised: 'Of course he wasn't there.'

It is accepted now without bitterness or resigned self-pity: 'I didn't feel badly.'

There is a sense of ease of mind and serenity that has been absent for long months. This acceptance makes it possible to 'lie and think about him', relaxed and comforted.

The pain of grief and misery of depression carry within them the seeds of healing. The grief and misery demand relief. It comes not by forgetting but by realising and accepting that the vital relationship that once existed with a living person cannot be retrieved; the companionship and physical presence can never be recovered.

When this truth is accepted, not just superficially but deep inside, then grief begins to ease. Perhaps for years there will be moments of illusion or wishful thinking in which truth will be submerged in fantasy, and when fact again takes over it will bring back bitterness and tears. As time passes however these episodes will become less frequent and less acute and will cease to be indulged as they become less satisfying.

This does not mean that mourners will not grieve any more. Sometimes years later memories will flood back and may bring tears or sorrow. Times of special significance, such as a birthday or the anniversary of the day of death or the wedding, may revive the pain and grief. Christmas too may be a sad rather than joyful time, especially if there are no children around to show their love and excitement and allay loneliness. But unhappy times are fewer, and further and further apart. Painful feelings lessen, so that the dead come to be remembered and talked about comfortably and even with delight.

In time, in the mourner's own time, the reality comes to be accepted: the dead have died; they will not come back; the past cannot be recovered; things will never be the same.

Some who have made a study of bereavement suggest that one year after the death the bereaved are generally beginning – but only beginning – to look forward rather than back, though when temperament and circumstances are favourable some may even reach a degree of acceptable contentment in nine months or so. Neither assessment is universally true.

There is clear statistically supported evidence that when death is sudden, unexpected or violent, recovery may take much longer, as much as four years or even more.

Others too may find that they need a longer span of time in which to complete their journey through the long dark tunnel.

There is no timetable for the human heart: its woes and joys do not work by any clock or calendar. Indeed, I doubt if most of us who have lost one we love could pinpoint an actual moment, day, week or month when we knew that our grief was done. Grief must not, cannot be hurried. If we are wise, we shall not strive to be cured nor keep taking a look within to see how we are getting on. We shall look outward and forward rather than back and discover that we can take the sudden heartache and searing memories in our stride as we gently welcome new activities, opportunities, friendships and interests. We have gained new strength as we have learnt to accept our loss. Life is now positively acceptable; it may even at times be fun!

Laughter – yes, *laughter* – returns. And there are few more encouraging, heart-warming signs of recovery than a good, spontaneous laugh!

Acceptance is a healthy, positive step forward. It does not happen all at once or once and for all, but gradually it brings a sense of sanity regained, of purpose and inner re-integration. It is a time of personal growth and outgoing opportunity, holding promises of peace and contentment, even joy.

Healing

Grief, always the result of loss, is the pain of *not having*. Through the suffering of grief – the yearning, fears, anger, guilt, depression and loneliness – we gradually learn to live without the one we have lost. We win through to an acceptance of our loss, to a freedom from *not having*. Then, and only then, we find healing, which is not only freedom from the pain of our loss, but a positive recovery of *having*.

The rather technical term 'internalisation' is used for the sense of possessing within oneself the presence of the essential reality of a loved person. A German psychiatrist defined it like this: 'The loved object [person] is not gone, for I now carry it with me and can never lose it.' The bereaved who have loosened the ties of the past and have accepted the loss of the physical presence, are now free to repossess in their hearts a conscious and comforting relationship with the one they love. The one who has died becomes part of the inner reality of the one who has deeply mourned. This is not something that can be very simply explained, but many will affirm this sense of inner containment and contentment.

For some there is an even greater joy: the presence of the loved one becomes a vital, lively experience. This is how C. S. Lewis recounts it: 'Just at those moments when I feel least sorrow – getting into my morning bath is one of them – she rushes upon my mind in her full reality . . . as she is in her own right.' And in a book quoted earlier in which, besides much else, Lily Pincus writes of her own bereavement, she tells of 'the tonic' of her husband's presence: 'It happens most often on waking . . . or at night when I go to sleep . . . and is a reassuring, gratifying experience which feels absolutely realistic.' It is, she adds, 'a wonderful surprise that this is increasing as time goes on.' St John Chrysostom, a bishop living in the 4th century A.D., knew about internalisation, though he had simpler words for it. 'He whom we love and lose', he wrote, 'is no longer where he was before. He is now wherever we are.'

This is the testimony of many; my hope and prayer is that what is written here may help to bring this rich and blessed healing to many more.

Appendix – Sources of Help and Advice

1. CRUSE is the national organisation for the widowed and their children. Her Majesty the Queen is its patron, and Cruse held its 25th anniversary in 1984. There are some hundred or more local branches throughout the country. If there is a local branch in an area its address and telephone number will be in the local directory, or the information service of the public library will tell you how to get in touch. If there is no local branch, write or telephone to the Cruse headquarters at:

   Cruse House, 126 Sheen Road,
   Richmond, Surrey TW9 1UR
   Telephone: 081–940 4818

   A local branch or the national headquarters will welcome any enquiry about bereavement and give information about nearest counselling services. Even for those with no special needs, membership is invaluable. Cruse publishes a monthly *Chronicle* for members, also other literature, including a useful holiday list. Local branches offer individual help and advice and a variety of social activities.

2. COMPASSIONATE FRIENDS is an international organisation of bereaved parents offering friendship and understanding to other bereaved parents. It has branches in various countries. If information is not obtainable locally, contact:

   The National Secretary, Compassionate Friends,
   5 Lower Clifton Hill, Clifton, Bristol BS8 1BT.
   Telephone: 0727 292778.

3. SANDS – Stillbirth and Neonatal Death Society helps parents who have experienced stillbirths and other perinatal and neonatal deaths. It has established a network of befriending

parents throughout the country and has set up well over 100 local groups. More information can be obtained from:

Stillbirth and Neonatal Death Society,
Argyle House, 29–31 Euston Road, London NW1 2SD.
Telephone: 071–833 2851/2

SANDS has produced a leaflet for parents who have suffered a perinatal death, which the Health Education Council has printed and distributed under the title *The Loss of Your Baby*.

4. CITIZENS ADVICE BUREAUX will be listed in local directories. The CAB work through trained staff to give reliable advice and help about most practical and social problems.

5. The SAMARITANS have branches in all large towns. In any crisis situation they can be contacted by telephone throughout the day and, in many places, during the night.

6. RELATE has many local branches manned by trained staff. They have proved very helpful to some widowed people concerning second marriages.

7. GAY SWITCHBOARD offers a bereavement counselling service for bereaved homosexuals.
Telephone: 071–837 7324 (24-hour service)

8. THE FOUNDATION FOR THE STUDY OF INFANT DEATHS has a network of befriending parents throughout the country to help those bereaved by the sudden death of an infant. Parents are supported throughout their subsequent pregnancies and with their next children. The Foundation also acts as an information and resource centre and has published a booklet entitled *Information for parents following the unexpected death of their baby*. Further information from:

The Foundation for the Study of Infant Deaths
15 Belgrave Square, London SW1X 8PS
Telephone: 071–235 1721

Suggestions for Further Reading

This list does not attempt to be comprehensive, but draws attention to some books presenting different aspects of the subject of bereavement.

GENERAL

All in the End is Harvest, ed. Agnes Whitaker. Cruse/Darton Longman and Todd, 1984.

Begin Again, Margaret Torrie. Dent, 1970.

Bereavement: Studies of Grief in Adult Life, C. Murray Parkes. Tavistock Publications, 1972.

Coping with Crises, Ruth Fowke. Hodder and Stoughton, 1968 (Marshall Morgan and Scott, 1983).

Coping with Depression, Myra Chave-Jones. Lion Publishing, 1971.

Death and the Family: the Importance of Mourning, Lily Pincus. Faber, 1976.

A Death in the Family, Jean Richardson. Lion Publishing, 1979.

Entry into Life, George Appleton. Darton Longman and Todd, 1985.

The Facts of Death, Michael A. Simpson. Prentice Hall (USA), 1979.

Forgetting's No Excuse, Mary Stott. Faber, 1973 (Virago, 1975).

Grief and How to Live with It, Sarah Morris. Allen and Unwin, 1971.

A Grief Observed, C. S. Lewis. Faber, 1961.

Letter to a Younger Son, Christopher Leach. Dent 1981.

On Death and Dying, Elisabeth Kübler-Ross. Tavistock Publications, 1970.

A Time to Die, Katharine Milne. Wayland Publications, 1977. (For school use.)
What to Do when Someone Dies, ed. E. Rudinger. Consumers' Association, 1978.

NOVELS

In the Springtime of the Year, Susan Hill. Hamish Hamilton, 1974.
Perfect Happiness, Penelope Lively. Heinemann, 1983.

PAMPHLETS

Death in Your Family, Russell Grigg. Rigby (Australia), 1978.
For Those Who Mourn, SPCK, 1982.
The Loss of Your Baby, Health Education Council.
What to Do After a Death, Department of Health and Social Security (Pamphlet 49).

PERIODICAL

Bereavement Care: for all who help the bereaved, edited by C. Murray Parkes and Dora Black. Cruse (3 issues a year).

*

TAPE

Through Grief, Elizabeth Collick. Mrs Collick has recorded a tape to help bereaved people, with the same title as this book. It lasts about 75 minutes, and covers nine different aspects of normal grief experience. Mrs Collick does not expect listeners to hear it all through at one sitting, but to use sections as appropriate. £3.50 plus 50p postage and packing. Available only from Cruse, 126 Sheen Road, Richmond, Surrey TW9 1UR.